# The Mommy Book

*by*
*Cheryl Salem*

**Harrison House**
**Tulsa, Oklahoma**

# Contents

# Dedication

To Daddy, my husband Harry Salem, who inspires me daily to be a better Mommy. I love you, Sweetheart. Thank you for believing in me.

# Acknowledgements

To my friend, Amy Denae Hossler, who continually pulled, pushed, challenged, and encouraged me through her tremendous writing talent and her close walk with the Lord, to finish this work for mommies everywhere. Thank you!

# A Letter From Cheryl to You

Dear Mommy:

I know you are busy and sometimes it's difficult to take even ten minutes a day to read, but you and your family are worth it. As you read this book, keep the following in mind.

1. Pray the prayers out loud.

2. If you have more than one child, read the Praying With Power sections with one child's name, then pray all the way through out loud with each consecutive child's name. (Or, take each child's name all the way through for an entire month, then the next month pray for the next child, and so on.)

3. I suggest you go though each devotional (one a day), looking up all the scriptures, underlining them, reading them aloud, and praying all the prayers out loud. At the end of 31 days start over and do it all again.

4. If you are a single mom, remember, the Father God will be your husband and a father to your children.

My prayer is that as you read the following pages, take faith action, and pray with power, you will be strengthened and encouraged in your pursuit of godly motherhood. Remember 3 John 4 (AMP): **I have no greater joy than this, to hear that my [spiritual] children are living their lives in the Truth.**

God bless you!

Cheryl Salem

# 1
# The Power of Impartation

*For I long to see you, that I may impart to you some*
*spiritual gift, so that you may be established.*

**Romans 1:11**

As Christian parents we have the ability and privilege
to impart spiritual truths into our children's spirits. Even
though they may not fully comprehend everything we read
or speak to them in the natural, their spirits receive much
more than we know.

To think about our children's spirits as being the same
age as ours is quite a revelation! Jeremiah 1:5 says *Before* I
**formed you in the womb I knew you.** The Word says God
knew you before you were conceived! How did God know
you? Were you a spirit walking around in Heaven waiting
to be born? I don't think so. However, before you were
ever conceived you were already in God's thoughts. He
was already thinking of you! You were already on His
mind. Our children's spirits (and of course ours too) are
eternal — not a "certain age"! Comprehending this
revelation will change our whole perspective on *imparting*
into our children's lives.

Webster's dictionary defines the word *impart* as "to give
a share of, make known, communicate." When we realize
that our children's spirits are able to receive so much at
such an early age (even in the womb), we will understand
the impact of the unlimited privilege we have to impart the
Word of God into them.

As we impart into our children by the Spirit of God,
they will comprehend great spiritual truths at an early age.
When our first son, Lil' Harry, was six years old, he asked

my husband Harry and me if he could receive "that Spanish prayer we pray every night." We explained that the prayer language he wanted was given by receiving the Holy Spirit into his life. Lil' Harry said "OK, I want Him." We prayed together, he believed, and he immediately began speaking in his heavenly prayer language. He uses his prayer language regularly without prompting from us.

Our son, Roman, is now five years old. If anything (and I mean *anything*!) is amiss, Roman will either say, "Mama, let's pray for it" or without hesitation he will simply lay his hands on the area and command the blessings of God to be in operation.

Lil' Harry and Roman have watched us in the natural and received spiritual impartation from us in the areas of receiving the Holy Spirit and knowing how to pray in times of need. Lil' Harry has shown a great longing to be close to the Father God, and we are so thankful he has received the power of the Holy Spirit early in his life. Both Roman and Lil' Harry know how to pray and expect results when they do so. It is vital that we impart God's Word and Spirit into our children.

Remember — we do not impart *what we know*, we impart *who we are*. Whether you like yourself or not, you are imparting yourself into your children every moment you spend with them.

## Praying With Power

*Father, I thank You for the power of imparting the Word of God into my children. I thank You that my children are capable of receiving Your truth in their spirits even from the womb. I thank You that as I ask for wisdom, You will liberally give it to me (James 1:5). I invite the Holy Spirit to come and guide me as a parent, teaching me the things I am to impart into my children. I give You the glory that my children will have great spiritual understanding at an early age and will impact Your kingdom in a mighty way. In Jesus' precious name, amen.*

## Taking Faith Action

Take a few minutes to ask the Father God to reveal several things He wants you to impart into your children. Write down three (3) specific things (or areas) that you feel impressed by the Holy Spirit to impart into your children. Ask the Lord to give you insight, discernment, and wisdom as to how to impart these specific things into your children, whether spiritual or natural.

(1)

(2)

(3)

# 2
# "Mama, Pray!"

People were bringing little children to Jesus to have him touch them, but the disciples rebuked them. When Jesus saw this, he was indignant. He said to them, "Let the little children come to me, and do not hinder them, for the kingdom of God belongs to such as these. I tell you the truth, anyone who will not receive the kingdom of God like a little child will never enter it." And he took the children in his arms, put his hands on them and blessed them.

Mark 10:13-16 (NIV)

So many of us pray only one time for God to heal something in our body and are absolutely depressed if the healing doesn't immediately manifest. Of course, God can and often does miraculously heal us the moment we ask. However, many times He allows our faith to be stretched and to grow in the process of receiving our healing.

Think about this...we are completely willing to go to the doctor and get an antibiotic prescription, take it three times a day for ten days, and not even expect to be well until our antibiotics are nearly gone. Why, then, are we too stubborn to press in consistently and persistently with the Word of God for our healing?

When our second child, Roman, was only two years old, the Lord gave me a beautiful illustration of why Jesus exhorts us to come to Him as little children. He awoke in the night very sick to his stomach, but instead of whining and crying, he was screaming something at us. We came running down the hall trying to figure out what he was saying. By the time we got to his room we had finally interpreted the words of his heartfelt cry.

He was sitting up in bed, violently sick. However, instead of feeling sorry for himself like so many adults would have in this situation, he was screaming, "Mama, pray! Mama, pray!" He came out of his sleep knowing what to do in a crisis. How many people do you know, much less a two-year-old, who wake up out of a deep sleep knowing to pray when something is wrong?

After we got Roman settled down and he fell back to sleep, he got sick several more times during the night. Each time he woke up screaming the same thing. "Mama, pray! Daddy, pray!" Even though his healing did not come immediately, he never changed his request. He never got tired of asking us to pray. He never said, "Why isn't God healing me?" He stayed consistent with his faith, his prayer, and his confession.

You see, in teaching a child how to believe, one of the most vital points is to teach them you never quit believing. *Never!!! You continue to believe until you have what you need from the Father, no matter how long it takes.*

Children learn more from our example than from our words. Words are important, but example is much more effective for lasting results. Our children know what God has done for me. They know God healed me (I was severely injured and crippled for years from a near-fatal car wreck) but they also know I had a short leg for a long time. They look at me now, completely healed and restored, and this teaches them to hold on to their faith no matter how long it takes to receive what they are desiring.

Just like Roman, we cannot look at our symptoms when we are praying for our healing. We must look to the Word of God and stand on His covenant promises. We must put God's Word into our hearts and minds and allow hope to grow. Hope is the blueprint for faith, and our faith will enable us to receive all that God has promised us. (Hebrews 11:1; James 5:15.) It all starts with coming to Jesus like a little child. When Roman awoke sick that night, he knew the only answer was prayer, prayer, prayer. He never quit requesting prayer. Why? Because he never doubted that God would answer!

## Praying With Power

*Father, forgive me for my "instant everything" mentality. I come to You as a little child and ask You to purify my heart and renew my childlike faith. I thank You, Lord, that faith is the substance of things hoped for, and I know that Your Word (Your covenant promises) will cause me to earnestly expect to receive from You. Father, give me a tenacity to hold on to and stand on Your promises regarding any area of my life. (Hebrews 10:35.) This moment I declare Your Word in Matthew 21:22 that says, "Whatever things you ask in prayer, believing, you will receive." In Jesus' name, amen.*

## Taking Faith Action

Think of several examples of God's faithfulness to you and take the time to share them with your children. Tell your children specifically how you prayed and believed God, and how He faithfully answered. Ask them to tell you about any prayers they have prayed and how God answered them. Take a piece of paper (or your prayer journal) and write down prayer requests and date them. Ask your children for any they would like to write down. Show them where you will write down the answer and the date that God answers. If your children are old enough, have them start their own "Answered Prayers" journal.

# 3

# A Prayer for Robyn

## by Jessye M. Ruffin

*By the anointing of the Holy Spirit Jessye wrote this prayer
for her daughter Robyn when she left for college.*

Lord Jesus, You are King over all the earth. For the
earth is the Lord's and them that are in it. Your
righteousness is the only government that the people of
God can live under peaceably. Your government redeems
our lives from delusion, oppression, fraud and violence;
and precious and costly is the blood of Your saints. Your
saints call You holy and bow at Your feet to be Your
handmaidens and vessels filled with Your honor.

As one of Your handmaidens, my daughter Robyn has
dwelt under the tent of Your righteousness and holiness all
of her born days. You have caused her to tabernacle
continually under the canopy of Your blessings. Her soul
cries out that You are a holy God Who judges and defends
the afflicted always. You have continually come to her aid
in the foreign land of Louisiana and have touched the
hearts of Your people to love and protect her. For this, my
heart is overwhelmed at the wonder of Your love and
faithfulness.

Truly, You are a God Who keeps covenant and keeps
Your children in foreign lands. Lord, I ask that You
continually deliver Robyn from the jaws of her enemies and
crush her oppressor at every hand. Let Your peace abound in
her life until the sun and moon are no more. Cause her to
flourish under your glory, Lord. As she goes about her day,
let her thrive on that campus, living a life of prudence and

discernment. Let godly wisdom set up a stronghold of defense in her and through her, touching the lives of those around her. Under the light of Your glory, let her see light and be a light for those around her to find You and Your way.

Robyn is one of the redeemed who is called by Your name, and may Your prosperity follow behind her closely. Overtake her with Your goodness and mercy, Lord. Let everything she sets at her foot and hand to do glorify your name forever and ever.

If it is on the track field, let her feet move with the grace of a gazelle who is running to meet the Creator of all things, the Lord Jesus. If it is jumping, let her jump as one whose longing is fulfilled by leaping to meet you in the sky. Let the winds be always favorable to her, giving her the push that she needs to cross the finish line first and always a victor to your glory, Lord. Let faith, hope, and love provide the passion to continually glorify Your name on the track, not only through performance, but godly conduct, character, and behavior, so that Your name will never be a reproach in Louisiana.

May the sword of the Spirit cut over all workers of unrighteousness who seek to defile and cause Robyn to live a life of compromise and rebellion. In relationships, cause her heart to revere and hear Your name, knowing that light and darkness have no fellowship together, for how can two walk together except they be in agreement. Your handmaiden, Robyn, was given to You at birth, so You, the Ruler and Savior of all things, are put in remembrance always to keep and preserve that which has been entrusted to You. Father, keep Your watchful eye upon her...delivering her out of every temptation and harmful situation. Send Your angels to fight the war in the heavenly places above her head, redeeming her from the influence of witchcraft, whoredom, antichrist, perversity, and lust. Holy Spirit, keep her and infuse her with Your power.

Let Your favor envelope her and set her up on the mountain of the Lord in regard to the authorities and teachers over her. Cause diligence and perseverance to seek her out and shower her with those reward only found in the kingdom of God and given to the righteous on the earth. Because your blessing is upon her, cause all who bless her to be overwhelmingly blessed for extending their hand to her.

Guard and keep her health and well-being, because You are the only physician who continually keeps and understands covenant. Robyn knows that it was Your saving stripes that purchased her divine health and it is because of this that, as a baby, she trusted no one else but You.

Robyn's passion has always been to love and serve no other but You Who keep covenant through all generations. In the midst of Your holy place, she has always found a shelter and refuge in Your lovingkindness and mercy. Earnestly remember Your handmaiden and fill her heart continually with worship and her mouth with praise. Let her not forsake the gathering together with other believers in Your Church, so that the wolf will have no victory over one lonely sheep. Blessed be your glorious name, Lord Jesus, because you rule in Robyn's life and reign over the whole earth. Amen.

*Jessye M. Ruffin is a wife and mother of two grown children in Flower Mound, Texas. She heads the counseling department of Covenant Church in Carrollton, Texas, and is a frequent speaker in many circles. Jessye feels one of the highest callings of a godly woman is that of mothering not only her own children but God's children through the precious tool of mentoring.*

# 4
# God Has a Plan

**And He shall not judge by the sight of His eyes, nor decide by the hearing of His ears.**

**Isaiah 11:3**

We need to remember that many wars won in the spirit realm may *look like* defeat to the natural eye. If we have survived and are standing when the dust settles — we *are* the winners and Satan is defeated. Hallelujah!

The one left standing at the end of the war is the winner. We may be beaten up pretty badly, we may have a few scars or some wounds that are bleeding, but if we are standing — we are the winner!

The Father emphasized this point to me when Lil' Harry was four years old. We were opening our first retail store, and he was with us when we were at the location getting everything ready. As usual, he was climbing on things, and he climbed up on a metal cabinet and pulled it over on himself! It fell full force across his chest and face. He was seriously cut and had to have several stitches across his cheek and under his nose.

I said to the angels, "Where were you guys? Were you on a coffee break or something?" I was really angry with them. I have seen angels over the years and not only do I know they exist, I know they work for us on this earth. It made me so angry when I thought those angels just stood around and let that metal cabinet fall on my precious baby's face! It was more than I could fathom that they would allow that to happen.

Several days later, after I had calmed down and realized I do not own my children, nor can I interfere with God's plan for their lives, Harry pointed out to me that the angels had saved Lil' Harry's life. I began to feel a peace and a calm come over me. I felt an assurance that the Father had it all under control. My job was to relax and quit trying to run the show. Isaiah 26:3 says, **You will keep him in perfect peace, whose mind is stayed on You, because he trusts in You.** When I got my focus back on Jesus, perfect and constant peace began to rest on me. *Then* I could hear from God!

I am not saying God caused the cabinet to fall on Lil' Harry. What I am saying is we do not know the plan, and we cannot predict what it is going to take to mold us into the men and women of God we are to become. Remember, when things go wrong, God always has a way of deliverance for us.

After I got my mind back on track, God showed me how the angels *were* working to protect Lil' Harry. The doctor even said the cabinet should have crushed his chest, broken his cheek, or put out his eye. Thank God our faith is not moved by the way things look! I began to realize the angels had been on duty after all. They were *not* on a coffee break, and they *had* saved Lil' Harry's life.

## Praying With Power

*Father God, thank You that Your plans for my children and me are good (Jeremiah 29:11). Thank You that You have a divine plan for each one of my children's lives. I realize that You are sovereign and You know what it takes to mold me and my children into the men and women You have created us to be. I claim Your Word in Isaiah 11:2-3 that says, "He shall not judge by what he sees with his eyes (the way a situation looks!) or decide by what he hears with his ears," but I will discern situations by the Spirit of the Lord Who is in me.*

*Thank You that scars don't mean I am defeated and that You will always give me the strength to be standing at the end of any battle. I claim that strength for my children and pray that they will always be standing when the dust from the battle settles. In Jesus' victorious name, amen.*

## Taking Faith Action

Pray the armor of God over yourself and each one of your children. If your children are old enough (even if they are not, let them watch and listen to you), teach them the following scripture. As you do so, visually act out the putting on of God's armor. (Example: Putting on the helmet and tightening a belt, etc.) Teach them to pray this daily, and of course, we as parents *must* do the same!

Therefore put on the full armor of God, so that when the day of evil comes, you may be able to stand your ground, and after you have done everything, to stand. Stand firm then, with the belt of truth buckled around your waist, with the breastplate of righteousness in place, and with your feet fitted with the readiness that comes from the gospel of peace. In addition to all this, take up the shield of faith, with which you can extinguish all the flaming arrows of the evil one. Take the helmet of salvation and the sword of the Spirit, which is the word of God. And pray in the Spirit on all occasions with all kinds of prayers and requests. With this in mind, be alert and always keep on praying for all the saints. (Ephesians 6:11-18; author's paraphrase.)

Put on the whole armor:

Belt of Truth (Protects the emotions, soul)

Breastplate of Righteousness (integrity, moral rectitude, and right standing; protects your spirit)

Feet shod with Peace (Protects your steps and direction)

Shield of Faith (Protects your body)

Helmet of Salvation (Protects your mind)

Sword of the Spirit (Not just to protect, but also an offensive weapon)

Pray at all times (This is your prayer cloak, raincoat, wrap)

*Notice, there is no armor to cover the backside, so there must be no retreat or you could get shot in the tail-end!*

*Notice, the spirit, soul, and body are completely protected!*

# 5
# Psalm 91 Protection
## by Lynn Braco

**No harm will befall you, no disaster will come near your tent. For he will command his angels concerning you to guard you in *all* your ways.**

**Psalm 91:10-11 (NIV)**

I can remember watching our son Paulie drive into the woods behind our house, excitedly waving as he rode his snowmobile through the fresh-fallen snow. He was off for an afternoon of winter fun, going riding with a dear friend who was one of the men in our church. I felt very confident of his safety when he was with this wonderful man of God. Just moments before he left, I remember reminding him to be extra careful, and I prayed the promises of Psalm 91 over him.

I had so many errands to run that I took my list and went on my way. It was certainly a perfect winter day in New England. The streets were freshly plowed from the snowfall the night before and the accumulation over the past few weeks was at least two feet.

I carefully went from place to place accomplishing all I had to do and then headed home, planning dinner and the evening's activities as I drove. When I pulled into the garage, I met my husband who was pulling in also. I was so glad to see him. I had a trunk load of bundles and groceries and I welcomed his help! As we walked into our breezeway and approached the side entrance, there in a puddle of water was a pile of soaking wet clothes, boots, hats, and gloves. We both yelled, "PAULIE!"

We dropped the groceries and began to call out, "Paulie, Paulie!" He was not home. Neither was the snowmobile. Something was terribly wrong! It was dark and very cold out. Where could he be? We began making phone calls. After reaching two or three answering machines, we were finally successful in getting a "real" person on the phone who told us there had been an accident! Paulie had gone through the ice on the pond of a golf course and the snowmobile went under the ice! The person did not know where our son and our friend were.

Now this is where the *benefit* of the implanted Word of God kicks in. It was a *"way of life" for us to pray over our children every day and to declare the Word into their lives.* This day was no different. The Word was in, above, and around our son. I declared the promise of Psalm 91(NIV) to him, especially verses 10 and 11: **Then *no harm* will befall you, no disaster will come near your tent. For he will command his angels concerning you to guard you in *all* your ways.** I honestly believe that my son's angels, who I commissioned that morning, were getting a real run for their money chasing him through the snow.

Apparently, when he went up a big mound of snow and came over to the other side, he crashed through the ice of a small pond. Our friend and some other people were able to speedily lift him up and help him get to shore through the frigid water. Then our friend hurriedly put Paulie on his own snowmobile and brought him home to change. He made a few calls to get the snowmobile out of the pond before it froze over again.

We hadn't a clue all this was going on — not even a note. So we prayed and asked the Holy Spirit to lead us to where the accident took place and it was as though we had written directions! We made a few left turns and a few right turns and there in a dark field off in the distance, we could see lights, a tow truck, and a plow. We shifted into four-wheel drive and made haste. We couldn't get there fast enough. What a delight to see our *son — whole, unharmed, and unshaken!*

What a difference when we make a *daily covenant with the Lord for our children.* I believe this could have been a terrible catastrophe, but *it was minor* because of a daily family lifestyle that included *commissioning the angels to protect* our seed. It's amazing to see the results of *applying the Word of God to the lives of our children.* He will *perform His Word over our children,* but we must first *take the time to sow it into them.* A harvest of *deliverance, protection, good health, intelligence,* and *sound minds* will come. Our son Paulie is living proof of that.

*Lynn Braco is the wife of Paul Braco and the mother of two children. She also has one grandchild. Lynn is co-pastor with her husband at Parkway Christian Center in New England. She is a National Women's Conference speaker with testimony after testimony of "standing" on God's Word and seeing miracles take place in her household and her church!*

# 6
# Resting in the Father's Love

**Come to Me all you who labor and are heavy laden, and I will give you rest.**

Matthew 11:28

As we become parents, we begin to see a tiny glimpse of the true love the Father God has for us. Our children made me aware of this truth because I realized they completely accepted me just as I was. I don't have to perform for them — they love me anyway. Our children have a way of making us feel loved no matter who we are or what we do or don't do. The love from our children is irreplaceable, yet the love of the Father God is greater still. God brought me to a beautiful understanding of His unconditional love during the pregnancy of our third child.

When I was pregnant with Gabrielle, our daughter, I was confined to bed rest for seven months because of complications. For the first time in my life, I couldn't travel and minister (or do housework either!) so I was forced to "rest." You see to me, just sitting still before the Lord seemed so unproductive. I couldn't imagine God ever being happy with me just lying there not producing — much less Him *wanting* me to just be still and know that He is God (Psalm 46:10). I had lived my life trying to be productive to please everyone around me, including God. I had not grasped the truth that God loves me regardless of what I can or cannot do for Him.

I had planned constructive tasks to do as I lay confined in bed such as writing a book on our children. Yet as I tried to accomplish those things, nothing would happen. I couldn't get started. My creative juices just wouldn't flow. I couldn't seem to get it together. The only thing I could write was, "Why is it when you are in a crisis you can't create?" Ha! This was not like me at all! I was always getting more accomplished than anyone else I knew. Now, all of a sudden I was just floating along accomplishing *nothing*. I was beginning to get frustrated and angry with the whole situation.

Finally, I went to God and He began to talk to me (He would have talked to me earlier, if I had gone before Him instead of trying to make things happen on my own). He told me He wanted me to rest before Him. He was not impressed with my schedule, nor was He moved by my "busyness."

The Father began to impress upon me that His love for me was not measured by how much I did for Him. *He loved me if I never did another thing for Him. God loved me if I couldn't* ***do*** *anything!*

You might be thinking that any idiot should know this. But for some reason, I had lived for God and loved Him all these years, teaching everyone else that God's love is unconditional — yet it never dawned on me that I really didn't believe God's love was unconditional for *me*. I thought I had to do all that was humanly possible for Him to continue to love me and use me for His kingdom. What a revelation to finally comprehend God's love for me. The Father God loves me. He loves *me!*

From then on, I spent many hours every day alone with my Father God. All I wanted to do all day was read His Word, talk to Him, be quiet before Him, and just simply rest in Him. Oh, how good it felt to lie in His arms and know He loves me and likes to be with me, even more than I like to be with Him.

## Praying With Power

*Father God, right now I will be still and know that You are God. Right now I receive Your unconditional love. I thank You that I don't have to perform — You just love me exactly as I am. I thank You that no matter how much or how little I do, Your love for me remains the same.*

*I realize that as a parent I am an expression of Your love to my children. I ask Father, that **You pour Your love through me** to my children, so I may love them unconditionally. I bind the spirit of performance in my life and in my children's lives in the name of Jesus. I loose liberty (2 Corinthians 3:17) and rest (Matthew 11:28) over my family and me. Thank You that I can rest in You, know I am loved, and be an expression of Your love to my children. In Jesus' name, amen.*

## Taking Faith Action

Think of three (3) areas where you feel you have to "perform" in order to be loved (by family, friends, mate, God):

*For Example:*

(1) *Our home (clean, neat, organized) — Super homemaker*

(2) *Our children (disciplined, obedient, cutest, smartest, most talented)*

(3) *My appearance (looking like Miss America 24 hours a day)*

(1)

(2)

(3)

Take the three areas you listed above and picture yourself laying those areas on the altar of God and then "see" yourself free. Stake your claim that you are loved regardless of your "performance" in these areas and give God the glory for the victory.

Now write down three (3) areas where you might be tempted to require your children to "perform" :

(1)

(2)

(3)

Remind yourself that you do not love your children based on their performance (just as God doesn't love you based on your performance). Ask your children for forgiveness if you have offended them. Pray that God's unconditional love will infiltrate these areas and flow through you into your child.

# 7
# "Hold You Me"

**Out of the mouths of babes and nursing infants
You have ordained strength.**

**Psalm 8:2**

Have you ever felt like screaming out, "I have nothing left to give!"? Of course you have — we all have. Sometimes we feel as if all we do is give, give, give to everyone around us (especially as moms!). However, God has such a wonderful blessing for us as parents. Our *children* can give to us. If we will open our eyes and *receive* what they have to give, they will bless us beyond measure!

When Roman was about two years old, I saw the blessing of our children "giving" to me. When he wanted me to take him in my arms, he would come running up to me and grab me around the knees saying, "Hold you me." He not only wanted me to hold him, but he also wanted to hold me! Children want to give of themselves to us just as we want to give of ourselves to them.

I am winning the fight, but recently I have fought exhaustion on a daily basis. Children know when you can barely put one foot in front of the other — especially when your normal speed is high gear! The last few months Roman has been slipping out of his bed in the middle of the night and coming into our room. He ever so quietly slips to my cheek, and says, "Mommy, I love you." I ask him if he needs anything, and each time he says he just wanted to tell me he loves me. He will never know how that refreshes, revives, and energizes me.

Children love us like the Father God — unconditionally! I don't have to be a great star to be loved by my children.

They love me because I am "Mommy" — God loves me because I am His child. There is nothing like the love of a little child. So often a parent has never been loved on this earth the way their child loves them. The Father God can pour His love into our hearts through our children and minister to us in great ways.

God uses Lil' Harry to give me strength; He uses Roman to give me joy; and He has used Gabrielle to bring me emotional healing I didn't even know I needed. I believe my children will bring strength, joy, and healing to me for the rest of my life. God even used Malachi Charles (our baby who was miscarried) to give me a greater compassion. One thing for sure, the love of our children is an example of the pure love of the Father God. Children are able to touch our hearts so deeply — we just have to be willing to receive from them.

Maybe that is one of the reasons why Jesus said, **Let the little children come to Me, and do not forbid them; for of such is the kingdom of heaven** (Matthew 19:14). Not only did Jesus bless the children — I'm sure they blessed Him. Jesus wanted the children near because He knew the power of receiving a child's love.

## Praying With Power

*Jesus, You love the little children. I can almost see You smile as You "took them up in Your arms, laid Your hands on them, and blessed them." (Mark 10:16.) Children are so precious to Your heart. When You walked the earth, You wanted them to come close to You. You wanted to hold them and bless them. Thank You for loving the children.*

*I ask that Your tenderness, love, and compassion flow through me toward my children and pour over them. I ask that You give me an open heart to receive from my children what You have placed within them to give to me. Allow me to see the refreshing love that You will bless me with through them. Thank You,*

*Father, that through my children I have felt and experienced an example of the purity and glory of Your unconditional love. In Jesus' name, amen.*

## Taking Faith Action

Take the time today to gather your children (or child) up to you and tell them you know that God uses them to bless you. If your children are old enough, ask them if they would like to lay hands on you and pray for you. Give each child a turn. Whether they thank God for the puppy or whatever (don't correct a thing!), after they pray exhort them and thank them for giving of themselves to you. Tell them they have such a giving spirit. Then lay hands on them and bless them.

# 8
# Big Humor From a Little Boy
## by Jeanne Caldwell

**A merry heart does good, like medicine.**
**Proverbs 17:22**

One day when my son, Ronnie, was about two years old, I took him over to my mother's house for her to keep him for a few hours. While he was there, my younger sister, Rhonda, took him outside to play. While they were playing, a "yellow jacket" started buzzing around them, so Rhonda quickly killed it before they got stung!

When I came to get him, he ran out to meet me yelling, "Momma, come and see the *yellow-overcoat* Rhonda killed!" Needless to say, we had a big laugh.

It seemed Ronnie was always mixing up his words like that. One time he had eaten "squash" at his grandmother's, so when I cooked it a few weeks later he said, "I don't want any of that *smash*." We laughed again. He was a great pleasure to have around — most of the time!

Enjoy your children — God gave them to you to make you laugh!

*Jeanne Caldwell is the wife of Happy Caldwell and the mother of one child. She also has five grandchildren. She is the co-founder of Agape Church, which includes a television network, churches, and Bible schools around the world. She is an ordained minister, recording artist, and is the author of a new book titled* **Learning to Trust God's Faithfulness***.*

# 9
# Strength Is Not a Weakness!

**The God of Israel is He *who gives strength* and power to His people.**

Psalm 68:35

When a child has a strong personality we sometimes see him or her as difficult. We tend to be tougher on them, which is not always the best way to handle a strong-willed child. I was definitely harder on Lil' Harry (our first son) because of his strength. I had to learn that strength is a great asset in his life and it is up to me *to cultivate it, not destroy it.*

Lil' Harry is the physical image of his father, so my problem with Lil' Harry was not his looks! It was his nature, personality, persistence (stubbornness), and tenacity — everything *but* his looks. He reminded me of me! Absolutely me in every way!

It was like looking into a mirror and seeing myself the way I really was before I learned to hide behind the manipulative traits life taught me. Oh, what a traumatic thing to realize, there is someone on this earth so much like me!

I could barely stand living with *me*, trying to figure *myself* out and survive my *own* driving nature, much less to realize there is a carbon copy of me! And a male one to boot!

I wanted Lil' Harry's life to be perfect — everything I wanted my life to be, with no mistakes, no trials, no tribulations, and no problems. This is what I wanted for Lil' Harry. I wanted his life to be absolutely the opposite of mine — trouble free. Sounds good, doesn't it? How many of us know how unrealistic and impossible that is?!

Lil' Harry has to have the freedom to grow up, make his own choices, and become who God called and created him to be. *This was not my second chance in life to correct everything I had done wrong the first time around.* No! No! That would be completely unfair to him. It would never work. Obviously, the Father God taught me (and is still teaching me) about myself through Lil' Harry. I love our son very much. I am thankful for him and the things God is teaching me through him. No one could ever love a child more or be more thankful for a child than I have been for Lil' Harry.

Proverbs 22:6 says in the Hebrew, **Train up a child in the *bent in which he was created*, and when he is old he will not depart from it.** The very things that will make Lil' Harry a strong man of God are the traits that need bending (not breaking) toward God. We are to work with God's design for our children, the way He created them to be.

So it is important to look at a child's strong personality as a *strength* and not a *weakness*. While that very strength can push you "to your limit" on stressful days, it is the same strength God will use in a positive manner for his/her destiny in life. Remember, God created your child with a strong drive for a reason.

As you seek the Lord for wisdom and guidance in training your strong-willed child, the Holy Spirit will guide you in channeling that strength in God's ordained direction. As you diligently cultivate your strong child with the help of the Holy Spirit, you will see a beautiful strength from the Father God blossom in him/her. As I have seen in my own life, the child with a strong personality will bless your heart beyond measure.

## Praying With Power

*Father God, I praise You that _____ is fearfully and wonderfully made, and marvelous are Your works. I thank You for the strong personality that You have put in _____. Thank You that I now see this strength as positive. I invite You, Holy Spirit, to come into this situation. I thank You that You will direct and assist me as I cultivate this God-given strength in _____. I give You the glory, Lord, for this precious, sensitive, and strong child. In Jesus' name, amen.*

## Taking Faith Action

Write down several different areas where you have seen your strong-willed child as difficult. Submit these areas to the Lord and allow the Holy Spirit to reveal to you how they are positive! Write down several ways you can encourage your child to use his/her strength in a positive way. And remember, the very traits that seem so difficult to manage in a parenting situation may be the traits which will make that child a strong leader for God.

# 10
# Uniquely Designed...
# Uniquely Destined

May He grant you according to your heart's desire,
and fulfill all your purpose.

**Psalm 20:4**

As I was comparing the personalities of our three
children one day, it dawned on me that the Father God has
made all of us so different. No two individuals are exactly
the same. We are unique to the Father. We bring Him great
joy, strength, and happiness, just like our children bring me.

Each child has their own way of doing things, their own
personality, their own strengths, and their own weaknesses.
This diversity is what makes children fun, challenging,
frustrating, and wonderful. Having three children so
uniquely different showed me one more aspect of the
Father's personality and His character. *God loves individuals,
not clones.*

God has been teaching me to love all people for who
they are (not trying to make them like me to be correct). If
people are different from us (example: laid back, instead of
driven), it does not mean that we are right and they are
wrong. In the same way, our children do not have to be like
us, feel like us, or think like us to be correct. If two people
agree on everything, then one of them is unnecessary!
Proverbs 27:17 says, **Iron sharpens iron.**

We need to accept every person around us (including
all of our children) for the way they are — not imposing our
own personalities on them. The Father God likes the unique
little quirks that make us who we really are. Seeing the

precious difference in our three children (and how God so diversely made our personalities) was just one more insight into the beauty of our Heavenly Father!

The truth is, there are few set rules or absolutes in child rearing. All children, and I mean *all children*, are completely different. You cannot rear them the same, discipline them the same, feed them the same, potty train them the same — *nothing is the same*. Lil' Harry challenges me and gives me great strength. Roman is pure joy and love except for sometimes having a "morning attitude" and bad temper. Gabrielle has brought healing in every area of my life. Each child brings different blessings and different challenges.

Just when you think you have it all figured out here comes the next one, and everything is different. God should give us a manual with each child. I guess in a way He did, the Bible, but that manual is generic and applies to all "models." Praise God for the Holy Spirit! He takes those generic instructions and helps us apply them more specifically to each child.

Every child is uniquely precious. Each child is born with a particular purpose and destiny — designed by God. The Father God has divinely placed personalities, gifts, and talents in our children to accomplish those plans for their lives. Let's enjoy the differences and nurture our children's individual personalities — allowing them to be all that God has created them to be.

## Praying With Power

*Father, I thank You that _____ is created with a unique personality, anointed gifts, and particular talents to fulfill the destiny that You have for his/her life. Thank You, Father, that You have given the Holy Spirit to teach us how to individually train and nurture this child. Your Word says, "There are diversities of gifts, but the same Spirit" (1 Corinthians 12:4), and I give You the glory for the gifts You have placed in my child. In the name of Jesus, I call forth every gift to fruition that You have placed in my child. I thank You, Father God, that _____ will fulfill his/her purpose on this earth. Help me to thoroughly enjoy and genuinely encourage every aspect of _____ 's personality, gifts, and talents. In Jesus' name, amen.*

## Taking Faith Action

Take time today to thank God specifically for your child's personality, unique talents, and anointed giftings (individually name them). See his/her uniqueness as a blessing, not a curse. Allow the Holy Spirit to spotlight any areas you have been too busy to notice in your child. Take time to observe how wonderfully God has designed your family!

Be sure to verbally affirm your children (and spouse for that matter) as to how special God has created them! Take the time to sit down with each child, look them in the eyes, and read Psalm 139:13-16 out loud to them. (This will be good for you to hear for yourself as well!)

**You made all the delicate, inner parts of my body, and knit them together in my mother's womb. Thank you for making me so wonderfully complex! It is amazing to think about. Your workmanship is marvelous — and how well I know it. You were there while I was being formed in utter seclusion! You saw me before I was born and scheduled each day of my life before I began to breathe. Every day was recorded in your Book!**

**Psalm 139:13-16 (TLB)**

# 11
# Four *Different* Children!
## By Carrie Prewitt  (Cheryl's Mother)

When we were bringing up our children, we never dreamed of going anyplace that our children could not go also.  If there was a school function, cake walk, carnival, singing in the church, or even a death in the community — everyone attended, including the children!  If it wasn't a place for everyone, no one went!  We did everything as a family.

We endeavored to show our children that love could *cure* anything.  Love was *always* the key.  It *had* to be with four wonderfully different children, each uniquely designed by God!  Our four children (Paulette, Cheryl, Tim, and Heath) had to be dealt with in four different ways.

You could just look at Paulette, point a finger at her, and she would be quiet as a mouse.  Cheryl was very easy to control as well.  I don't ever remember giving her a spanking.  (She didn't pay me to write that!  Ha!)  Cheryl was always real sweet.  Her brothers said she was too sweet and that she could "butter up" anyone!  Cheryl learned early in life that if she was practicing the piano I wouldn't make her do any chores — so practice she did!  And there's not a lot of mischief you can get into on a piano bench (Ha!).

Now on the other hand, Tim had to have a spanking almost every day.  If he missed one day, the next day he would have to have two to make up for it!  He was what most people call a "true little boy."  Everyone needs a "true little boy"!  Our other son, Heath, never had any spankings until he was four or five years old.

51

Heath was severely injured in the car wreck that almost devastated our family. From that injury, Heath developed epilepsy and crying would trigger the epilepsy. Therefore, we all catered a little more to him, especially until he was completely healed by the Lord when he was almost five years old.

Hosea and I had four children with four completely different personalities. I thank the Lord for Paulette, Cheryl, Tim, and Heath, each one precious and special in his/her own ways.

*Carrie Prewitt is the wife of Hosea A. Prewitt (who went to be with the Lord May 2, 1994) and mother of four children (including Cheryl! I love you, Mom!). Carrie and Hosea have spent their lives teaching and training their children to follow God, hear His voice, and do His will.*

# 12

# A Little Wine for Mama

So they were all amazed and perplexed, saying to one another, "Whatever could this mean?" Others mocking said, "They are full of new wine." But Peter, standing up with the eleven, raised his voice and said to them, "Men of Judea and all who dwell in Jerusalem, let this be known to you, and heed my words. For these are not drunk, as you suppose, since it is only the third hour of the day. But this is what was spoken by the prophet Joel: 'And it shall come to pass in the last days, says God, That I will pour out of My Spirit on all flesh.'"

Acts 2:12-17

I grew up in a precious little Methodist church in Choctaw County, Mississippi. I learned all about God's love and what Jesus has done for me. I received Christ as my Lord and Savior in that church but there was no Holy Spirit presented there. We had a duet in our church instead of a trio!

As I grew up in the Lord and received the Holy Spirit at a Kenneth Hagin meeting, I discovered a whole new realm of walking with God. There was only one problem. I had never overcome my conservative roots when it came to worshipping the Lord.

Those of you who know me are probably saying, "You must be kidding! You, conservative?!" I was very free with my praise and even with my worship, but not with myself! I could give God all of my life. I could praise Him and give my testimony in any situation regardless of how uncomfortable it might be. But to give my whole being — body, soul, mind, and spirit — was just a little too much for me, especially in public.

What if I made a fool of myself? What if God asked me to dance, or shout, or *run* for His glory?! Heaven forbid!

The one thing I had always asked God from the beginning of my ministry was, "Please God, don't make me be weird!" Aren't we silly? We say to the Father, "Take me, use me whatever way You want, but please don't do it in a way that might embarrass me in front of the world!" Isn't that ridiculous?! God does not make us weird, but He does tell us that when we belong to Him we will be a peculiar people — set apart for His glory. We may seem different from the world. That is because we *are* different. We belong to God, and He has made us *uniquely* His own. (Titus 2:14.) There is such a freedom in being one-hundred-percent God's!

One thing about our Father, if He has a yielded vessel He will do whatever is necessary to free you before Him. Everyone is not set free in the same way. In my case, I had to lose my pride and become a "fool" for Christ. I use the word "fool" carefully, because from what I have experienced there are enough fruits, nuts, and flakes in the Body of Christ to open a granola factory. However, there is a difference between being a "plain ole fool" and being a "fool" for Christ.

God is looking for the person who is willing to risk it all, to completely let down his barriers, and trust God even to the point of being "beside himself." I want to be that person. That means I can't worry about appearance or how the people around me see me when I worship my Father God.

I have finally come to the point where I can completely trust God and "let my spiritual hair down," but it took a spiritual "drunken" experience for me. Now I know firsthand what delighting myself *in the Lord* really means. First, with my mind I choose to be happy. Second, I allow the Holy Spirit to overtake me. I get so completely wrapped up in Him that I act, look, and feel like they must have on the day of Pentecost in Acts, chapter two (when the people looking on thought the entire crowd was drunk on wine).

I don't know what it feels like to be drunk on earthly wine, but I do know what it feels like to be drunk on the heavenly wine of the Holy Spirit — and I wouldn't trade the freedom I have experienced for anything in the whole world. Try it! You'll like it!

Why am I talking about "letting your spiritual hair down?" Because as mothers, we deal with a huge amount of stress. Most of the time we operate in overload physically, emotionally, and mentally. Mothers *need* the "new wine of the Holy Spirit!" We need God's rest and peace!

You see, the world turns to alcohol to experience a temporary escape from their problems or pressures. This is a counterfeit of God's rest and peace. The world's solution has many drawbacks, from a hangover to no lasting peace when it is all over.

However, when we have given ourselves completely over to God and the Holy Spirit, there are no side effects, no hangovers, and no drawbacks. There is nothing like being full to overflowing with the Holy Spirit. The Holy Spirit will cause you to walk in God's rest and peace as you relinquish complete control to Him. Let the Holy Spirit take control and drink deep from God's refreshing "new wine." Ephesians 5:18-19 says, **Do not be drunk with wine, in which is dissipation; but be filled** (controlled by) **the Spirit, speaking to one another in psalms and hymns and spiritual songs, singing and making melody in your heart to the Lord.** This wine will greatly enhance motherhood and bring a wonderful freedom to your life!

## Praying With Power

*Father God, thank You that You have not made me weird, but peculiar, and set me apart for Your glory. I claim Your Word in 2*

*Corinthians 3:17 that says, "Now the Lord is the Spirit; and where the Spirit of the Lord is, there is liberty." I trust You, Lord, and I am willing to be "beside myself" if necessary, to be free in You. I relinquish control and I ask You, Holy Spirit, to fill me with "new wine" so I may be refreshed and free. Father God, I want to be so overcome with You that I am drunk in the new wine of the Holy Spirit. Thank You for the freedom that I have in Your Spirit. In Jesus' name, amen.*

## Taking Faith Action

Write down ways you might be keeping yourself from receiving the "new wine" of the Holy Spirit. Pray through each area and *release* it to the Father God. Totally surrender yourself to the Holy Spirit and receive all that God has for you. Spend time praising and worshipping the Father God right now. Stay in the atmosphere of His anointed presence until you are refilled and refreshed.

When you start enjoying God daily you can relax and have fun and your children will *see* and feel a difference in you. Children want fun and excitement in their lives. The Holy Spirit is fun and exciting when we finally give up control and let Him *lead*!

# 13
# The Supermom Syndrome

**For You will light my lamp; The Lord my God will enlighten my darkness.** *For by you I can run against a troop, by my God I can leap over a wall.* **As for God, His way is perfect.**

**Psalm 18:28-30**

Sometimes we mothers feel like we have a huge "S" emblazoned on our chest. It really is quite amazing how we do what we do. Of course, being a mother myself, I can talk this way. When you became a mother, did you suddenly have a new-found respect, love, and compassion for your own mother? It changes your whole perspective, doesn't it? Being a mother is the most challenging and rewarding work in the world. And just like anyone else, we can get caught up in the "performance trap."

Do you measure your success as a mother based on your performance? Are there times when you feel frustrated and can't seem to "get it together"? Are you trying to be a "Supermom"? Are you involved in so many activities that none of them are allowing quality time for just you, your husband, and your children? So many mothers feel exasperated and unworthy because they are trying to be a mother in their own strength. Many women struggle to be the "perfect mom." Yet God has not called us to be perfect mothers.

Many of us battle with the dreamy picture we had when we were younger that *we* would be the perfect mom! We would always look absolutely stunning, have our house sparkling clean, prepare gourmet meals, and dress our children adorably (matched to our outfit of course!). We would awaken in the morning to sweetly sing to our babies as we serve coffee to our smiling husband, who is putting on the shirt we have freshly starched for him. Our days would be filled with walks in the park, Bible stories with the kids, and tea time with other wonderful mothers.

Unfortunately, on most days reality is not quite that perfect — loads of laundry, demanding schedules, frustrating time restraints, and no slowing down at all. You do not sit down all day long! Not even to eat lunch! The pros far outweigh the cons, but it is easy to slip into the "Supermom syndrome." Everyone wants something from you all the time. And if no one else is asking you to "perform" — you pick up the slack and heap self-expectations on top of the real-life requirements. When we realize we are not perfect (and don't have to be), there will be even greater joy in parenting!

When I became a mother, I quickly learned I was not perfect. I had to learn to prioritize every minute to insure I spent proper time with my husband and our children. To be quite transparent, I love to work — to travel, minister, and sing have always been my first loves. However, the Father God began to show me that what I was doing was great and effective, but my family could not suffer for the Gospel's sake. God would never destroy a family to promote a ministry.

I began to see the greatest thing I could ever do was to train up our children in the way they should go, so that when they were older they would not depart from God. (Proverbs 22:6.) I received insight into the fact that if I taught our children to love God, hear His voice, and follow His lead — I would be accomplishing more in the long run than I could ever do on my own. The idea of reproducing the call of God in our children has to be the most satisfying revelation God has ever given me. Our children are our living testimony that goes on after us. Through them we can then bless generations to come! Genesis 12:3 (AMP) says, **In you** (or your seed) **will all the families and kindred of the earth be blessed [and by you they will bless themselves].**

Without the help of the Father God you cannot be the wife you need to be, successfully train and love your children, and fulfill God's purpose for your life. There may be days that your house is less than perfect and your meals quite plain, but every moment is precious as you train and impart into your children. Through the help of the Holy Spirit you *can* be a supermom for your children. You just need to take off your red cape and realize that you are completely equipped and anointed through Jesus to be a mother. After all, God hand-picked you and your children and put you together. You were made for each other — and God believes in you both.

## Praying With Power

*Father, I praise You and worship You. Thank You for believing in me enough to entrust* _____ *to me. I give You the glory for divinely placing him/her and me together in this child-parent relationship. In the name of Jesus Christ, I bind the spirit of performance in my life and loose rest and competence through Christ. I claim Your Word in 2 Corinthians 3:4-5 (NIV) that says, "Such confidence as this is ours through Christ before God. Not that we are competent in ourselves to claim anything for ourselves, but our competence comes from God." Thank You that I can do all things through Christ who strengthens me (Phillipians 4:13) and that You truly think* **I am a supermom!**

## Taking Faith Action

If you are not in the habit of doing so, take the time today to plan out the next week. Schedule out basics, such as meals and laundry on particular days. However, also schedule in "special" time for your children, a couple of "special" meals, and even some refresher time for yourself (exercise too!). Prioritize other activities and events around this schedule. Use this as a guideline and not a guilt trap!

Give plenty of time for each activity so as not to be rushed. Ask the Holy Spirit to lead and guide you as you plan. Ask the Lord to make His desires your desires. Always remember to put your time with Him first and all these other things will be added unto you! (Matthew 6:33.)

# 14

# Use What You've Been Given
## by Lindsay Roberts

I love music and I've always loved to sing. But anyone who has ever heard me sing knows that I am not a singer. Even my children know that their mother can't sing.

A few years ago, Jordan was having a nightmare. As I went into her room, I thought, *Oh, you sweet little thing. If I can just do something that's familiar, it will soothe you.* I held her and began to softly sing, "Yes, Jesus loves me."

Jordan stopped screaming, looked straight at me, and said, "Oh, Mother, please don't sing!"

I thought, *Well, if Jordan doesn't appreciate my singing, Olivia will.* Later as I held Olivia in my arms and began singing to her, she looked up at me with a sad little face and said, "Mommy, don't cry!" I had an immediate revelation of what my talents are and what they definitely are not!

God has given each one of us our own unique talents in areas where we can really excel and let our light shine. I may not be much of a singer, but I can soothe a baby to sleep faster than just about anybody I know! And that's something I'm proud of. God gave me that talent and I use it with joy.

Don't disdain the talents that God has given to you. Like the wise servant in Jesus' parable who invested the talents his master gave him and received even more, look for ways and opportunities in which to use your God-given talents . . . whatever they are.

*Lindsay Roberts, first lady of Oral Roberts University, was called by God to stand beside her husband, Richard, in his capacity of President of Oral Roberts University and Oral Roberts Ministries.*

*A devoted mother, her life is busy raising three lovely daughters. Still, she finds the time to host the daily television program, A New Perspective, with her husband, Richard. She also serves as editor of the Daily Blessing publication and was appointed to the ORU Board of Regents.*

*"I am dedicated to God and willing to do whatever He calls me to do, "Lindsay says. "I also stand in support of the call of God upon my husband. He and I are both very grateful that God is using us for His glory."*

# 15
# Speaking and Praying the Word

**And these words which I command you today shall
be in your heart. You shall teach them diligently to
your children, and shall talk of them when you sit in
your house, when you walk by the way, when you lie
down, and when you rise up.**

Deuteronomy 6:6-7

I want to make sure our children know how to walk in
God's promises. I want them to know they can trust their
Father God to always be there for them. I realize we cannot
just sit down and read the *King James Version* of the Bible to
them and expect them to listen and be interested, but we
can talk the promises of God in our everyday conversation.
We can pray the promises of God out loud when we pray
over our children. They *are* listening. You might be
surprised what children absorb.

As parents, we endeavor to monitor our words so that
negative things do not come out of our mouths. Let's go
one step further — determine to speak the Word of God on
a regular basis. Let God's Word be the bulk of our
vocabulary. After all, our children learn most of their
language and vocabulary from us.

When your children present problems to you that they
want you to solve (in my house this happens all day long!)
learn to answer them with the Word of God. You can't say
"thus says the Lord," but you can say "the Bible says this
about your problem, or I think Jesus would want you to do
or say or choose this." You can give them some spiritual
food for thought when you tell them what to do.

You will not be able to answer your children with the
Word of God if *you* are not studying it on a regular basis.

Your knowledge of the Bible is vital in teaching your child. This in itself should be enough to motivate you to study, pray, and meditate on God's Word. You can do it! Your children are worth the effort it takes to learn. Get with it! It is never too late to get started. As you fill up on God's Word, it will overflow as you teach your children.

I teach my children how to pray the Word of God over themselves and over each other. We pray every night, "I anoint you in the name of the Father, the Son, and the Holy Spirit. I ask the Father to put four angels over you to guard, guide, direct, and protect you. I plead the blood of Jesus over you, under you, and all around you. I put a wall of prayer around you and a prayer covering over you." Depending on the circumstances of the day, I add to this prayer Isaiah 54:13, and all my children shall be taught of the Lord and great shall be their peace and undisturbed composure.

Psalm 91, in its entirety, is a good scripture to pray over your children. I insert our children's names one at a time in the place of "he." For example, "Harry (Roman) (Gabrielle) dwells in the secret place of the Most High and abides under the shadow of the Almighty. He will say of the Lord, You are my refuge and my fortress: my God in Him will I trust." Continue to read the entire scripture over each child until you feel peace in your heart that you have covered whatever situation they may be facing. Teaching your children to pray the Word of God at an early age is vital to their spiritual maturity and survival in these last days.

The challenge we face as parents is to consistently put the Word of God into *our* hearts and confess it with *our* mouths. We have all heard our words come out of our children's mouths! Let it be the *Word of God* coming out of our mouths that they repeat. How gloriously uplifting to hear the Word of God coming out of our children's mouths because of our constant confession of God's Word!

# Praying With Power

*Father God, I thank You that "Your Word is sharper than any two-edged sword" (Hebrews 4:12). I ask You, Father, to give me an unquenchable desire for Your Word. I thank You that as I give attention to Your words, incline my ear to Your sayings, not letting them depart from my sight, and keeping them in the midst of my heart...that Your Words will be life to me and health to my flesh. (Proverbs 4:20-22.) I claim Isaiah 55:11 that says, "So shall My word be that goes forth from My mouth... It shall accomplish what I please, and it shall prosper in the thing for which I sent it."*

*Holy Spirit, I ask that You come alongside me to help me recall the Word I put into my spirit, so I may speak and confess the Word of God more. Let me be so full of God's Word that it is natural for me to respond to my children with Your Word.*

*I pray that _____ will love the Word of God with all his/her heart. I pray that he/she will see the example that I set and desire to know and keep Your Word from a very early age. I pray that You will give _____ understanding and revelation of Your Word even as a small child. In Jesus' precious name, amen.*

# Taking Faith Action

Turn in your Bible to Psalm 91. Write out the entire psalm and leave blanks to fill in your child's name where it is appropriate. Example:

"_____ dwells in the secret place of the Most High and shall abide under the shadow of the Almighty.

"_____ will say of the Lord, He is my refuge and my fortress; My God, in Him I will trust."

Writing out this entire psalm will help put the Word into your spirit. Begin to meditate and memorize this entire passage and pray it over your children daily (and your spouse and yourself!). It may take a little longer to pray each individual's name in the entire chapter, but once you have done this several times, for several days in succession, you will find you have not just memorized the chapter, no — even better — you *know* the chapter!

Teach it to your children and have them pray verses over each other. Fill yourself to overflowing with God's Word, let it flow into your children, and then they will begin to impart God's Word into others.

# 16

# Word Blessings

## by Peggy Capps

**It is the Spirit who gives life; the flesh profits nothing. The words that I speak to you are spirit, and they are life.**

**John 6:63**

Have you ever heard a parent make the statement, "You are the meanest kid I have ever seen. I don't know what I am going to do with you!"? I have, and then watched it come to pass, just like they said. Notice in the Old Testament men blessed their children with *words*. In Genesis 49, verses 1 and 33, Jacob spoke words over his sons. When he finished commanding them, he gathered his feet up and died. The scripture called this prophecy!

You better watch what you prophesy over your children! Say good things to them and about them. Moses blessed the children of Israel with words in Deuteronomy 33:1 and it all came to pass just as he spoke it. *Be sure to speak **good** things over your children.*

*Peggy Capps is the wife of Charles Capps. She is the mother of two children and the grandmother of two. Peggy is the vice-president and office manager of Charles Capps Ministries.*

# 17
# Trained to Reign

**Train up a child in the way he should go, and when he is old he will not depart from it.**

**Proverbs 22:6**

We as parents are to train (not raise) our children. It is important to know what training means, so that we can be effective in training our children. One of the best definitions of training that I have found is in Richard Fugate's book, *What the Bible Says About Child Training:*

*Training* means "the process by which the one being trained is caused to show the results of the training." Therefore, child training is the process used by parents that will cause a child to reach the objective for which he has been trained.

*Raising* a child is not training. Plants and animals are raised. To raise something means to grow it. To raise a child would only consist of feeding, clothing, and protecting him from destruction until he reaches physical maturity. While it is true today that most parents are only "raising" their children, raising does not constitute the training of the soul that God intends.

Also, parents do not train their child by just telling him what they expect of him. Unless the child actually arrives at the point of functioning on his own in conformity to what he has been taught, he has not been trained. Parents can't have comfort in saying, "I just don't understand why he turned out this way. I always told him what was right." Telling is not training.

We Christian parents are to train our children by putting the Word of God into them. When we put the Word of God into our children it will take root because God's Word is alive and full of power. (Hebrews 4:12.) We are to be obedient to God and do what He has taught us to do — *train up a child!* The spirit in the child will grab hold of the Word of God and run with it.

Training is not something you do once or twice in a child's life and expect it to take root. You have to do it over and over again. When someone is training an animal to do tricks, they will work with that animal for hours on end, day after day, sometimes week after week, just to learn one trick.

Yet we humans expect our children to be able to grasp what we want them to learn with very little effort on our part. Training is as much hard work for the trainer as it is for the one being trained. It takes patience and endurance. This is the only way training can be effective.

When it comes to our children, we need to learn to give them our time — not just quality, but also quantity. Repetition is a great teacher. Don't get discouraged. Don't give up. Stick with it. Their little lives are worth it! Not only are your children important for this day and hour, but your children are vital for the years ahead!

I sincerely believe God is training up this younger generation to reign in the latter days. All that we impart into our children through the Holy Spirit and train into their spirits by the Word of God will enable them to be victorious in this world. With all diligence we are to train our children to love and serve the Lord with all their might — for our children are destined for greatness. Our children are the spiritual pillars and leaders of tomorrow. (Joel 2:28.)

Our son, Lil' Harry, asks me every time I am getting ready to leave on a ministry trip, "When are you going to let me go and preach?" I tell him when he is ready he can go. I'm sure it won't be too much longer. His heart is so open to the Father God. Lil' Harry is so sensitive to the voice of the Father. (I'm sure Roman and Gabrielle will be too!) *You train them and God will do the rest!*

## Praying With Power

*Heavenly Father, I give You honor and glory and thank You that You have given me the necessary information in Your Word to effectively train my children to love and serve You all the days of their lives. Holy Spirit, I welcome You into this training experience with _____. I ask, Father God, that You give me patience and endurance as I train him/her for Your glory. I claim James 1:5, which says you will give me wisdom when I ask for it. I thank You, God, for giving me Your wisdom for training my children. In Jesus' name, amen.*

## Taking Faith Action

Ask the Father what destiny He has for your child. Pray that the Holy Spirit will guide you into specific ways you can nurture and train your child for the call that God has on his/her life. Call forth the destiny God has ordained for your child every day, and bind the enemy from interfering with God's plan for your child's life in any way. Continually speak to your child that he/she is destined for greatness in the kingdom of God — and that God has a specific purpose for him/her to fulfill on this earth. Continually tell your child that you know he/she will love and serve the Lord all the days of his/her life.

# 18
# Nothing But Blessings!

**I call heaven and earth as witnesses today against you, that I have set before you life and death, blessing and cursing; therefore choose life, that both you and your descendants may live.**

**Deuteronomy 30:19**

Have you ever caught yourself saying something that your mom said to you a thousand times? Or what about realizing that you were preparing a certain meal exactly the way your mother did? It is amazing to see how much our parents have affected our behavior patterns. It is quite awesome to realize that we too are passing down many of our mannerisms and quirks to our children. And just as we pass things to our children in the natural realm, we also pass things to our children in the spiritual realm. We have the ability to pass generational *blessings* to our children, but we must also break every generational *curse* that could be passed to our children.

The Bible says in Exodus 20:5 that it is possible for the iniquity (sin) of fathers to visit upon children to the third and fourth generations. This is why it is very important that we sever any generational curses from our children.

I have learned more about the severing of generational curses since I became a mother. The one thing most of us want for our children is the very best they can possibly have — physically, mentally, emotionally, socially, and financially — I don't want our children carrying around any excess baggage from previous generations.

It's in our hands as parents to make sure they are protected from things in the past. We have the right to rebuke Satan and command him to get his hands off God's property. Satan cannot stay and hang onto our lives after he is exposed and his power is broken. Therefore, he cannot go into the next generation and harass them either — at least not as a generational curse passing from us to our children.

You might be thinking, "This Cheryl Salem has gone off the deep end." But let me show you what I mean. When you go to the doctor's office for a routine checkup, the first thing you have to fill out is a medical history of you and your relatives. You have to declare every illness from three generations back. By the time you have filled out this medical history, you are afraid of getting everything from migraines to cancer. *All Satan has to do is get you in fear thinking about what could be coming, and he has an open door to enter your body and life.*

There is no reason to be in fear about generational curses. We just need to be cognizant and in the name of Jesus break any curses that could be passed to our children. I want my children to be free from the past so they may soar like an eagle for the Father God. There will be nothing passing down from Harry (my husband) or me into any of our children except blessings, blessings, and more blessings! (Deuteronomy 28:2-14.)

## Praying With Power

*Father God, I plead the blood of Jesus over _____.*
*In the name of Jesus Christ of Nazareth, I renounce, reject and disown all of the sins of my ancestors from him/her. Holy Spirit, I ask that you reveal to me any areas in my life where I have allowed strongholds to be built that need to be pulled down and demolished in order to stop any generational curse from being passed to _____.*

*I claim 2 Corinthians 10:4 that says the weapons of our warfare are not carnal but mighty in God for pulling down strongholds. I thank You that the grace and blood of Jesus are sufficient to overcome any plan of the devil. Father, I pray that You will fill me up completely with Your Holy Spirit so my children will receive nothing but blessings as their inheritance. In the mighty name of Jesus, amen.*

## Taking Faith Action

Spend time today thinking over any areas which seem to be prevalent within your family — even several generations back where Satan could buffet your child (i.e., fear, divorce, abuse, disease, etc.). Ask the Holy Spirit to direct you in this. Write down each area and pray, breaking each generational curse over your child. Do some family history investigating, but remember not to get into fear or condemnation.

For example, perhaps you find that your mom, her mother, and her grandmother all continually dealt with serious discouragement and depression. Don't allow it to go another generation! Call that stronghold down and replace it by loosing the spirit of hope and faith! Stand on this verse: **And they overcame him by the blood of the Lamb and by the word of their testimony, and they did not love their lives to the death** (Revelation 12:11).

# 19
# *Never* Give Up!

**But as for you, brethren, do not grow weary in doing good.**

**2 Thessalonians 3:13**

I have decided that Satan is rather stupid, because he never seems to know when he is defeated. He just keeps coming back for more punishment and defeat. *That is why we children of God must never get weary in our well-doing.* If we do, then the ole devil has a chance to get a lick in on us. Don't give him this opportunity! He only deserves our heel on his head, crushing him to the ground!

You might be thinking, "You're right, but how do you keep going when you are so exhausted and need a rest?" The joy of the Lord is your strength! *If you haven't tapped into the power of getting into God's presence and experiencing the pure joy of the Lord, then you are apt to get tired and quit, which in turn is going to get your backside kicked by the devil.*

Harry and I learned this when Gabrielle was born. Due to complications, I had been in bed seven months with the pregnancy. By the time she arrived we were tired of fighting. Yet Satan just wouldn't leave us alone. We thought when we got Gabrielle here that we had finally won the battle and he would back off — but he didn't.

Satan didn't stop with a very difficult pregnancy. When Gabrielle was just a few weeks old we noticed she was having a problem with her breathing. When she was sleeping at night and sometimes while she was napping during the day she would just quit breathing. She had a condition known as sleep apnea. She would take a big hard breath and just not take another one.

At first we didn't recognize this as an attack of Satan, but it only took a short time to discover this was another one of his lies. It was back to fighting for our baby. We took all the necessary precautions with the doctors: tests, sleep monitors, etc. Finally, after taking authority over the devil repeatedly, Harry and I were in agreement that Satan was completely defeated. This occurred one night as we were getting ready for bed.

I had hooked Gabrielle up to the sleep monitor and laid her in her infant seat for the night. (She slept on the floor in her infant seat right beside me.) As I was preparing to go to bed the news was on. I wasn't paying any attention to it, then suddenly I heard that a baby had just died in a hospital because a staff person had hooked up a sleep monitor incorrectly! I panicked! I thought, "God, if a trained nurse accidentally hooked up this monitor incorrectly and killed a baby, how can I be sure that I am doing this correctly?"

I wasn't sure what to do for a few moments, so I talked to Harry and we closed our eyes and prayed in our prayer languages. After only a few moments we knew what we were to do. We called the doctor, discussed what the Holy Spirit had told us to do, and he was in agreement with our decision. We went over to Gabrielle, got her up, unhooked the monitor, and had it removed from our home.

Our faith, not our fear, had finally kicked into gear! Now we could truly believe God that she was healed, and Gabrielle hasn't had another attack on her breathing since! The whole experience reminded us that we can't ever let up where the devil is concerned. We have to stand our ground and not give him an inch. (Ephesians 6:10-18.) *He is counting on us to get tired and weary and then give up.* We have to remember what the Bible says about warfare in Ephesians.

Read the verses in Ephesians 6:10-18 out loud to yourself. Let your own ears hear you say, **and having done**

**all, to stand. Stand therefore, having your loins girt about with truth** (Ephesians 6:13,14 KJV). What does this mean to you? It should mean that no matter what Satan comes up with, God has commanded you to stand — not to sit down, lie down, or quit! Stand! Stand! Stand! This is a simple instruction in winning. It's called tenacity. Hold on, no matter what it looks like — no matter what the facts say.

We gird our loins with truth, not facts. This is where so many well-meaning Christians miss it. They hear the facts spoken by the world, reporters, doctors, circumstances, and situations — and they gird their loins with facts. This is the surest way I know of to fall and quit. God does not say for us to base our faith on the facts. He says to gird ourselves with the truth, not the facts. The truth is, facts are subject to change, and the Word of God stands forever. All we have to do is stand on God's Word in a situation and eventually the facts must line up with the truth. (Psalm 119:160.)

The doctors told us the facts about Gabrielle. They said she might not survive past six weeks because of the sleep apnea. We could have based our faith on those facts, but instead we chose to base our faith on what God's Word says about healing. We chose to believe the truth instead of the facts! Facts can kill you. Facts can take your hope and faith. But God's truth will always set you free!

I don't know about you, but I am tired of letting Satan pull me around by the nose! He doesn't have a right to my life, my family, or my ministry. He doesn't have any rights to anything! I am taking back what God has given me by choosing once again to believe God's truth instead of the circumstances or facts that surround my life. This is a good time for you to stand up and declare to the devil that he is the loser and you are the winner. Proclaim out loud the promises of God (1 John 4:4, Psalm 91, Isaiah 54:17). Resist the devil and he will flee as if in terror! (James 4:7.)

## Praying With Power

*Father, I come to You today and enter into Your glorious presence to regain my focus and receive fullness of joy (Psalm 16:11.) I have become tired and weary in the battle and I need Your strength and rest. Your Word says "the joy of the Lord is my strength" (Nehemiah 8:10) so I ask You to fill me to overflowing with Your joy. I ask for joy inexpressible (1 Peter 1:8.) Thank You Father God that I don't base my faith on the facts but on the truth of Your Word. Thank You that the Holy Spirit will help me to hold on to your Word no matter what any situation looks like. Satan, I serve you notice\* that because of the blood of Jesus you have no right to me, my family, my ministry, or any other area of my life. I stand on the truth of God's Word and know that His truth will make me free! (John 8:32.) In Jesus' victorious name, amen!*

\*When a notice or a summons is served by a duly authorized agent of the court system, it is a written document with a promise that a certain action must stop (or a certain action must follow) and that the highest authority in the land will back up the written document.

When we serve Satan notice that he must stop an action or release a situation, he must do it because it is backed up by God's Word, God's promise, and God's authority over him! Praise God!

## Taking Faith Action

List any circumstances in your life that look impossible according to the facts. List those facts, and then list the truth in God's Word. Search the scriptures prayerfully until you find the truth about your situation. Use a Bible concordance or topical promise book if necessary. Ask the Holy Spirit to make God's Word come alive in your spirit so that you will base your faith on God's truth instead of the facts.

| CIRCUMSTANCE | FACTS | GOD'S TRUTH |
| --- | --- | --- |

80

# 20

# Family Time

## by Evelyn Roberts

> And these words, which I command thee this day,
> shall be in thine heart: and thou shalt teach them
> diligently unto thy children, and shalt talk of them
> when thou sittest in thy house, and when thou walkest
> by the way, and when thou liest down, and when thou
> risest up.
>
> Deuteronomy 6:6-7 (KJV)

In today's world so many of us live in the fast lane that it's hard to take time to be with our family. This is especially difficult for working mothers. I know in our economy it is sometimes necessary for mothers to work to help make ends meet, but I wish it were not so. Children need to have their mothers and fathers close, to answer their questions, explain what's going on in the world, and help them feel protected and cared for.

So many school children come home to an empty house. They've had a hard day at school and there's no one home to talk to. Yes, children have hard days just like adults, and instead of kicking off their shoes and sitting on the couch to unwind like adults do, they want to talk to Mommy and Daddy about what happened today.

"Mommy, why did Johnny kick me?"

"Why won't Annie play with me?"

"Mommy, am I ugly?"

Suppertime used to be a time when everyone talked about their day and each child got his turn. Today so many

81

families never sit down to supper as a family — so *after school time* is missed, *suppertime* is missed and when bedtime comes, Mommy is too tired to listen to her child's plea. There has to be an answer for this if our children are to grow up to be normal people.

The Bible says, "Train up a child, " and this *takes time.* Mothers and fathers, I strongly encourage you to find time for your children — not just quality time as we hear so often, but *quantity time.* They need you!

*Evelyn Roberts is the wife of Oral Roberts and the mother of four children. She is also the grandmother of thirteen. Mrs. Roberts says about her ministry life, "I have been a helpmate to my husband in the ministry for 56 years. We have had an exciting and sometimes exhausting life...but I love it!"*

# 21
# Mom, God Believes in *You!*

Above all, love each other deeply, because love
covers over a multitude of sins.

1 Peter 4:8 (NIV)

How often since we have become mothers have we said
(or thought!), "Oh, I hope I'm being a good mother — I
hope I am doing this right!"? From the day we found out
we were expecting a baby, we began to paint a "perfect
parent" image and plan for a "perfect child." Oh, we all
agreed with the advice that "kids would be kids," but
inside *we just knew we* would be "perfect parents" and have
"perfect children." Not only were we *expecting* a baby —
but we began to put *expectations* on ourselves that not even
Mrs. Cleaver (on "Leave It To Beaver") could handle! We
didn't realize that our zeal for parenting would not keep us
from making mistakes.

Well, as reality would have it, when I became a mom, I
made mistakes too. My husband, Harry, has said to me
repeatedly, "lighten up, Frances!" (I don't know why he
calls me "Frances" — maybe just to make me laugh!)
Maybe if we can lighten up a little and look at the lighter
side of our being a parent, we can relieve some of the
pressure we put on ourselves and our children. Yes,
parenting *is* a serious responsibility, but we need to
seriously *enjoy* it, too!

The key is to be God-pleasing parents instead of people-
pleasing parents. Then we will have a completely different
perspective. When we are concerned about what others
think of our parenting skills, we create an impossible (and
miserable) pursuit of perfection for ourselves. Or, if we

place the pressure of perfect performance on our children, we can cause them to feel that they are only loved conditionally. Instead, we should be faithful to what the Father God wants us to do and be as parents, and be honorable to our children.

I learned the hard way that I needed to "chill out" about the "hard core" expectations I had placed on myself and our firstborn son, Lil' Harry. (Firstborns seem to get the brunt of many of mom's mistakes!) One afternoon while we were on a trip in California, Lil' Harry (two years old) and his cousin Jordan (three years old) were outside by a pool with my eleven-year-old niece, Trish. We adults were busy inside.

For the past few weeks we had been dealing with Lil' Harry about pushing others, something we would not tolerate. All of a sudden, Jordan was splashing and flailing in the swimming pool, squealing "Harry pushed me!" Of course, Trish jumped to the rescue and retrieved the soaking wet Jordan from the pool.

In a flash (*before* I thought) I immediately reacted, picked Lil' Harry up, and pitched him right into the water! I guess I thought that was the instant cure for pushing little girls into the swimming pool. (Ha! What maturity! Poor firstborns!) Of course, Trish was still in the water and fished Lil' Harry out for me and he was fine. My mistake was that I didn't even give Lil' Harry a chance to defend himself. Whether innocent or guilty, he deserved a chance to explain the situation. Then I could discipline him fairly, based on the facts and not my own embarrassment.

My instant judgment was *not* like the Father who is so faithful and just to forgive us. (1 John 1:9.) Praise God! We may make many mistakes, but God will always forgive us and give us the opportunity to grow. Day by day with God's grace and mercy we can become the parents God wants us to be. I had made a mistake and I had to ask Lil'

Harry to forgive me. Throwing him in didn't teach him how dangerous his actions had been.

I definitely learned a big lesson from a big mistake. The truth is that sometimes we can be unreasonably hard on our children, *and* ourselves as their parents. No, we are not perfect — yet God *believed in us enough* to give us the privilege of being a parent. Our children need to know that we *believe in them,* no matter what they do or don't do.

Of course, we discipline our children and educate them, *but we don't love our children according to their performance.* God doesn't love us according to our performance as parents (Thank You, Father God!). God believes in us — regardless of our mistakes. And just as God uncon-ditionally loves us, we need to unconditionally love our children and believe in them *even when they make mistakes.*

## Praying With Power

*Father, Your Word says in Romans 9:16 (NIV), "It does not, therefore, depend on man's desire or effort, but on God's mercy." Lord, You know that I desire to be a wonderful mother and that I am making every effort to be the best parent that I can possibly be, but Your Word says that it does not depend on my desire or effort, but on Your mercy. So, Father God, I pray that You will pour out Your mercy over my parenting skills. I pray that Your mercy will cover my mistakes, and I thank You that Your grace is sufficient in all things for me as a parent.*

*Lord, I pray that You will help me to always be willing to ask for forgiveness from _____ as the Holy Spirit convicts me of my wrongdoing toward him/her. Thank You, Father, that I don't have to be the "perfect mom" and that You don't love me based on my performance. I bind the spirit of performance from myself and my relationship with my child. Help me, Father God, to unconditionally love _____ _____ the way that You love me. I ask that Your unconditional love will flow through me to* _____ *continually. In Jesus' precious name, amen.*

## Taking Faith Action

Write your child a note today telling him/her, *"I believe in you."* Hide it where they will find it at an unexpected time. If your child is not old enough to read, sit them down eye to eye and tell them that you believe in them and that you love them with all your heart. It's okay if they are too young to understand what the word *believe* means. Speak to their spirit.

Write *yourself* a note, *"God believes in me"* and put it somewhere visible to remind you that you don't have to perform to be a good parent or to be loved by God.

# 22

# The Mediator

**For I will contend with him who contends with *you*, and I will give safety to your children and ease them.**

**Isaiah 49:25 (AMP)**

As I was growing up, I took music lessons from a very precious lady, Becky Curtis. Not only was Mrs. Curtis my music teacher, but I adored and loved her as my friend. Music was my life and music lessons with Mrs. Curtis were priceless to me. Unfortunately, when I was in the sixth grade, one evening I "overheard" a conversation between my parents that broke my heart. My mother was telling my daddy that we couldn't afford $8.00 per month for my lessons with Mrs. Curtis anymore.

Well, I took it upon myself to approach Mrs. Curtis with the dilemma. Through my tears, I told her I couldn't take lessons from her any longer because my parents could not afford them. Mrs. Curtis comforted me and reassured me that she would make a way for me to continue taking music lessons from her. She said I could clean her music room or run some errands to pay for them. I was relieved.

However, in the next few days, Mrs. Curtis contacted my mom to let her know what she was going to arrange for me to continue my music lessons. My mom (who was totally unaware that I had overheard the conversation between her and my father and that I had spoken with Mrs. Curtis) was so heartbroken that I had been hurt by their conversation and taken the burden of the situation on *my* shoulders. We all realized that it really boiled down to a communication problem. Mom and I should have talked about how much I loved my music lessons and how important they were to me.

Then, my mother could have talked with Mrs. Curtis and made arrangements for me to continue.

I tell you this story because it *is so important to communicate with your children and to be involved in their lives.* We are living in a society where parents are becoming more and more detached from their children. Many parents drop their children off at school at 8:00 a.m. and pick them up at 4:00 p.m., knowing only their child's teacher's name and *maybe* the subjects they are taking. We must get involved and be active in our children's school. Maybe we can't be involved in PTA or other organized functions — but we can be individually involved.

Harry and I are actively involved in Lil' Harry's school life. Harry takes him to school, walks him to the classroom, and gets a report from his teacher daily. I try to talk to his teacher every day when I pick him up. I talk to every teacher, counselor, principal, and anyone else who is in contact with Lil' Harry at his school. I ask Harry's teacher things like, "How was the day?" and "What did you do?"

I walk the halls of Lil' Harry's school and pray and plead the blood of Jesus. I also anoint the school and classrooms with oil. Why do I do this? Because our children are our prized possessions! I cannot take lightly what is being put into our child's mind and spirit at school! I have to know that our child is being built up, taught responsibility, and loved. *I cannot afford to assume that all is well with our child at school. I have to be in the "know"!*

I also communicate with Lil' Harry every day about his day at school. I ask questions until I get *satisfying* answers. I don't just accept ambiguous responses. I want to be in tune with Lil' Harry and I make sure I listen to him as he talks to me. Then he will know I am genuinely interested. I don't just want to know *what* happened, but *why* things happened and how he felt about them. I want to know about Lil' Harry's life!

Roman is in preschool twice a week and he is totally different from Lil' Harry. However, Roman also needs Harry and me to be involved in what he is doing. Roman is the type of child that you never have to wonder if he had a good day — every day is a good day. Roman is never a problem and hardly ever gets into trouble. But you know what? He still needs our attention. He still needs for us to ask, "How was your day? What did you do today? Were you a polite young man today?" If only the "squeaky wheel" gets the grease, the perfectly working wheel will desire to "squeak" just to get a little grease!

Everyone, no matter what their personality, needs attention. Try to give all of your children (and your husband!) equal time, attention, and affection. Don't think that they are not aware. The bigger children notice when the baby always gets his or her way! This keeps the lines of communication open so you are able to mediate for your children in both natural and spiritual matters. In order to intercede for them you have to be aware of the challenges they're facing.

God has put us in an incredible position of intercession for our children. Not only are we to intercede in prayer, but I believe we are to intercede in their daily lives. We are the mediator (Galatians 3:20) between our children and the "secular" world (their teachers, counselors, principal). The word *mediator* means "a go-between, umpire, reconciler, arbitrator, intermediary." If children didn't need mediators, God wouldn't have made parents! As parents, we are to "go between" our children and those outside influences. It is so important that we begin to realize the beautiful way God has designed protection for His (our) children. Let's do our part and get involved in our children's lives. They are worth it!

## Praying With Power

*Jesus, I thank You that You are my Mediator. Thank You that You stand between my sin and the Father God. Thank You that because of Your shed blood I stand in righteousness before my Heavenly Father.*

*Father God, I ask that You give me wisdom and boldness to be involved in my child's life outside our home. Help me to walk in a spirit of discernment and to be in the "know" about his/her school. I pray that I never neglect the important and priceless responsibility of communicating with _____. I pray, Holy Spirit, that You will remind me to always take the time to listen to what my child is saying to me and give me insight into the activities in his/her life.*

*Lord, I lift up (the name of the school where your child attends) to Your throne right now and I plead the blood of Jesus over it. I ask, Father, that You send thousands of warring angels to encamp around the school. I thank You, Father, that You will have _____'s guardian angels cover him/her front, back, left, right, above, and beneath as he/she is at school. I pray now for (your child's teacher's name) and ask, Father, that You give him/her wisdom and love for _____. I ask, Lord, that You give me favor (Psalm 5:12) with _____'s teachers, principal, and other people who are in contact with him/her. I pray that we will be able to communicate freely with regard to _____.*

*Thank You, Father God, for helping me to be a mom who is in the "know." In Jesus' name, amen.*

## Taking Faith Action

### 7 Practical Steps for Getting Involved in Your Child's Life

1. Go through your child's backpacks with them (I'm not kidding! They put their most valued things in there!). Allow them to show you, explain, and go over what's in there every day!

2. Read everything that comes home each day.

3. Ask them direct questions and don't accept ambiguous answers.

4. Ask the teacher questions (Harry and I do every day!)

5. Ask the principal, counselor, and extra-curricular teachers questions about their progress.

6. Communicate with *all people* who deal with your children.

7. Don't assume the adults in your children's lives are always right. Your children may have a better handle on things than the adults! But make sure you show respect to all those in authority over your children, whether you agree with them or not. This way your child will learn to respect authority at every level, and a rebellious spirit will not develop!

# 23

# Do What You Know to Do!

**I have loved you with an everlasting love; I have drawn you with loving-kindness.** *I will build you up again and you will be rebuilt.*

**Jeremiah 31:3-4 (NIV)**

I have recently walked through the deepest valley of my life. In December of 1993, I literally felt like I could not find the other side of that deep valley. I have taught and preached on "choosing to be happy" for many years. Yet I (Mrs. "choose to be happy" herself) was depressed. Our infant daughter, Gabrielle, had sleep apnea and I was totally worn out due to the situation.

Even though God completely healed Gabrielle when she was six weeks old, she did not sleep well for about six months after that. As a result, for six months after her healing I never slept more than fifteen minutes at a time, which resulted in greater physical exhaustion.

Although I kept smiling, preaching, and singing, I lost my voice, and then began to drop weight quickly. I had severe headaches and was nauseated much of the time. I was under attack and needed prayer cover, yet I was too proud to ask because I didn't want to disappoint anyone.

I went to my doctor and he told me that I had a chemical imbalance in my brain which was causing depression and all the other symptoms. He ran all kinds of tests on me and nothing else surfaced. I kept telling him that I was not depressed! I told him that depression is what doctors diagnose when they can't find anything else wrong! So he prayed for me and told me that I would be okay — he was my *comforter.*

We went home to visit my family for the holidays. My sister told me I had to get some help, that I had better start facing the truth and start talking to people who could understand what I was going through. My sister was my *confronter*. Well, she made me so mad that I packed up my kids and husband and went home. However, when I got home I went before the Lord and heard the truth.

I told my sister-in-law, Lindsay, the truth over lunch one day. I admitted I felt like I was in a maze and I couldn't find my way out. It seemed as if I was looking down on myself in the maze and could see the exit, but I couldn't get to it. Lindsay talked straight to me, counseled me, and prayed with me. She was my *enlightener*.

Soon after that I received a phone call from Ricky Van and Betty Shelton. Ricky Van felt that he had a word from the Lord for me and he told his wife, Betty. Ricky and Betty did not know what I was going through, yet Betty encouraged Ricky to call and tell me what the Lord had impressed upon his heart. Ricky said, "*God said for you to praise Him in the midst of it all and that there is a reason for it.*" Ricky and Betty were my *encouragers*.

Harry continually held everything together for the family during this time, taking everything he could off of my shoulders. He couldn't heal me; only God could do that. But he did and said everything he knew to do and say to help me find my way back to the surface. He was my *covering*.

A few weeks later I heard from the Lord about my situation. *God told me to "do what I knew to do."* I told Him that I was — and it wasn't working! Yet over and over God kept telling me, "*Do what you know to do.*" So I went and pulled out one of my old Bibles and began to read in the margins, things I had written years and years ago. At the bottom of one page it said, "I'll die before I give up."

Soon, I began to read the scriptures out loud. As I read and preached to myself, a new fire came up in my spirit. I literally preached myself out of depression with His Word — and I found my way back to the Father. I found my way out of the pit of depression.

In retrospect, I realize that as my life became more hectic, I covered everyone else with prayer, but I forgot to pray for me. I prayed for our kids, my husband, my ministry, the people I would be allowed to minister to, world issues — everyone and everything — but I forgot to cover me! It is important to pray for yourself — for your physical, spiritual, and emotional health. We are not any good to anyone else if we are not covered with prayer and strong in the Lord!

What about you? Are you covering yourself in prayer? Do you feel as if you are in a maze trying to find your way out? Are you fighting depression? Are you in denial about depression? If you *are* experiencing the symptoms that I mentioned above, get before the Father God and ask Him to reveal the *truth* to you. Talk to someone that you trust and be transparent. If you have unexplained physical symptoms such as weight loss, headaches, and nausea — get some help. There is a way out.

The Father God loves you and will deliver you from depression. He will comfort, confront, enlighten, and encourage you as you seek His help. Fight your way back to God — choose to get out of the trap Satan has set to try to destroy your life. Run and fall into the Father God's arms. He is there ready to strengthen and build you up again. There is hope! There is healing! The Father God really does have your answer.

## Praying With Power

*Father God, I praise You for Your faithfulness to meet me at every point in my spiritual walk. Thank You that You are the God of inexpressible and glorious joy (1 Peter 1:8) and that Your joy is in me. I know that I have victory in every area of my life, including depression and that weeping may remain for a night, but joy comes in the morning. (Psalm 30:5b.) So Father God, I cry out as the Psalmist did in Psalm 42:5 (NIV),*

> *"Why are you downcast, O my soul?*
> *Why so disturbed within me?*
> *Put your hope in God,*
> *for I will yet praise him,*
> *my Savior and my God."*

*My soul thirsts for You, Father God. Holy Spirit, I ask You to comfort me and enlighten me. Lead me into truth as I seek God in His Word. I pray Lord, that You will encourage and strengthen me as I stand against this attack. I bind the spirit of depression and loose the spirit of joy and life into my soul in the name of Jesus. Thank You, Father, that I have found my way back to You.*

*I speak life and health to my body, soul, and spirit. I plead the blood of Jesus over me from the top of my head to the soles of my feet. I take off the garment of heaviness and put on the garment of praise. (Isaiah 61:3.) I put on the full armor of God (Ephesians 6:10-18) and pray the seven-fold spirit of God over myself. (Isaiah 11:2.) Thank You, Father, for reminding me to cover myself as well as my family, friends, and ministry. I give You the glory for the victory over depression. In Jesus' name, amen.*

# Taking Faith Action

## 5 Practical Steps/Exhortations for Fighting Depression

1. Cover yourself! (Quit being comfortable with being sick or depressed! Psalm 37:4)

2. Get back in the Word of God — *for yourself!* Not just to minister to others!

3. Pray in tongues. **He who speaks in a tongue edifies himself** (1 Corinthians 14:4).

4. Praise the Lord. Even when you don't feel like it. Praise no matter how bad you feel or don't want to — praise, praise, praise Him! Offer up a sacrifice of praise. (Psalm 37:4; 116:17) Fight till you get out!

5. Get under anointed teaching and preaching.

*You can't be any good to your family if you aren't any good to yourself. You deserve to be well in every way!* 3 John 2 says, **Beloved, I pray that you may prosper in all things and be in health, just as your soul prospers.**

# 24

# What Do They See?

## by Mrs. Oretha Hagin

**Follow my example, as I follow the example of Christ.**

1 Corinthians 11:1 (NIV)

We always endeavored to set the right example for our children as they were growing up, and I believe it has helped them in their own walk with the Lord.

Children watch their parents, and it is critical for you as a parent to set the right example. It is always a mistake not to walk in love, but it is an even bigger mistake to do it in front of your children. It is harmful to your child's well-being, for example, to hear you talk badly about and criticize others.

So much is imparted to a child by what he or she sees in you. If you sow bad seeds by gossiping and not walking in love, and your children see that, those seeds are going to grow in them as well. You can impart your attitude to your children because they believe what you tell them, and they will really think about and meditate upon the things you say and do.

Your children will respect you and will learn positive habits and attitudes from you when your words and actions are a reflection of your love for God and His Word. What better motivation is there for setting a godly example for your children?

*Mrs. Oretha Hagin is the wife of Rev. Kenneth E. Hagin, founder and president of Kenneth Hagin Ministries and* RHEMA *Bible Training Center in Broken Arrow, Oklahoma. She serves as Vice-President of Kenneth Hagin Ministries and has authored the book,* **The Price Is Not Greater Than God's Grace.** *Mrs. Hagin is the mother of two, grandmother of five, and great-grandmother of five.*

# 25

# "Fear Not" Promises

**For God has not given us a spirit of fear, but of power and of love and of a sound mind.**
**2 Timothy 1:7**

Fear. We all know what it is, and we all know we are not supposed to fear. Yet it seems that fear lurks around every corner, wanting to grab hold of our lives. Fear is one of Satan's biggest deceptions in our lives. If Satan can get us into fear, he can rob us of our joy and our destiny. Fear paralyzes us and keeps us in bondage — and as parents (especially mothers) we must choose not to operate in fear.

In general, women are more prone to have to fight fear because they are more emotional than men. Men are not exempt by any means, but Genesis 3:15 says that God has put war between the devil and women — and fear is one of those battles. Therefore, we women must conquer fear. So how do we "fear not"?

I believe we can overcome fear by exposing the devil's deception, choosing not to fear, praying in the Spirit, and using the powerful Word of God as our *offensive* weapon. The Father God will reveal all roots of fear and then through His power and love in our lives give us the victory over that fear.

When I became pregnant with Gabrielle (our baby girl), I came face to face with a buried fear that had held me in bondage for many years. I was abused as a little girl by someone I had loved very much. He was a very good man, but he had a very bad problem. For years I kept this deep, dark secret and felt God surely couldn't love me. This is why I worked so hard to win God's approval. I thought if I accomplished enough "things," then He would be proud of me no matter what had happened when I was a child.

The worst part was that I felt like little girls didn't have normal lives, that they were never safe from "good" people, much less "bad" people. I was really confused about who I could trust, and consequently trusted no one. I was comfortable with this wall in my life, and certainly was not ready to deal with the emotional pain of the possibility that someone could hurt my little girl. That is why I always believed I would have only boys! I just knew God would let me keep hiding from my fears. Was I ever wrong!

When Gabrielle was conceived I was sure the baby would be another boy. Harry would never hear of anything but "boy confessions." He was so sure all of our children would be boys, and that was fine with me.

We had an ultrasound in the spring and it showed the baby was probably going to be a girl. Harry was sure they were wrong, and I didn't want to deal with the fact that it might be a girl, so I agreed with him that they were probably wrong.

A few weeks later the doctor did another ultrasound, and this one showed for sure that the baby was a girl. This hit me like a ton of bricks! In my mind, girls didn't have normal lives. Girls didn't have a lot of hope to be what I called *normal*. Normal is an odd word, I guess. "Normal" to me meant no pain, no abuse, no confusion, no hurt, only a safe place to run and hide from anyone and anything that could destroy my life. I didn't want a child of mine to go through anything I had, so my answer was to simply not want a girl.

I went before God and said "God, are You sure?" Isn't that funny how we question God when we don't want to deal with something? Harry was really fine about having a girl, but he just wouldn't admit it at the time. As for me, the problem was more than gender. It had a much deeper root than girl or boy — the root of abuse. In my little girl subconscious mind I wanted to be a boy because I thought only little girls were abused.

But I also still held on to another lie of Satan that girls couldn't be called of God. As a little girl I had cried before God, wanting to be a boy because I felt His call upon my life. I believed only boys could be called to preach and yet I felt this uncontrollable desire to preach and minister God's Word to hurting people.

Now I realize that this strong longing and desire to be a boy stemmed from thinking not only were little girls abused and always vulnerable to attack, but boys were called to preach. I wished to be a boy so nothing could harm me! And if I were a boy, I could preach and fulfill God's call on my life. In my mind, all I could equate to being female was pain, mental and emotional crippling, and no opportunity to do what I felt called of God to do.

Of course, as an adult I see the "warped" Satanic thinking in all of this. Satan's desire is to pervert everything in our lives, including our sexuality, making us completely unhappy with who we really are, and making us think that God made a mistake in making us the gender that we are. What a lie! We are fearfully and wonderfully made and everything about us is just right!

I now realize that God's perfect plan was for me to be totally female (to preach, teach, sing, etc.)! I *had* to be female to fulfill God's plan for my life. How could I ever have been Miss America and given Him all the glory without being female?!! I am truly fearfully and wonderfully made just like I am, so are you, and so are our children!

Satan had lied to me about these things and kept me in fear over having a female child. I had to face the fact that God's will had to be fulfilled through this child I was carrying. I had no right to predict, confess, or wish for a certain sex of this child. All I had the right to do was carry this child in my womb, rear her in the ways of the Lord, teach her how to hear God's voice, and trust God enough to do His perfect will in her life. I had learned to trust God in my own life, but now He was asking me to really trust Him with our children. *All of our children!*

God says in Isaiah 44:2-3 that He will pour His blessing on my offspring if I will "fear not." It is important for our children that we do not walk in fear! Not only will fear stifle *your* life, it can rob your *children* of God's blessing. God has given us many promises of what He will do when we *"fear not."* Satan wants to get us into fear so that we will not walk in faith and receive God's promises. However, the Father God has not given us a spirit of fear, but a spirit of power, love, and a sound mind. (2 Timothy 1:7.) Therefore, *we have the victory over fear.*

To counteract the effects of fear thoughts, we must continually remember things that are in opposition to them. **God has not given us a spirit of fear** but He has given us a *spirit of power*, a *spirit of love*, and a *spirit of a sound mind!* These abilities (power, love, and sound mind) are from the Father God and are *for you!* They are weapons against fear in your life.

Faith is the exact opposite of fear. To *not* have fear, you *must* have faith. Romans 10:17 says, **Faith comes by hearing, and hearing by the word of God**. To have faith you must *read* God's Word. Read it regularly and consistently. Feed on the Word like you eat three meals a day! If you really desire to be free from fear, you must discipline yourself and meditate on God's Word. You can do it! You really can — so where do you start?

Start with Psalm 91, Psalm 37:4, John 14 (the whole chapter) and other scriptures that are discussed in this book. Then get yourself a concordance and begin looking up (and writing down) every "fear not" scripture! You will be amazed as you dig into God's Word and *focus* on His promises how fear will begin to dissipate in your life!

I believe God wants to turn our entire generation back to Him. I believe He is telling us to stop entertaining ourselves and start disciplining ourselves. God is not going to speak to us or give us direction through secular television shows, the news, secular books, or magazines. He will speak to us through His Word and through prayer!

## Praying With Power

Let's make some declarations through the Word, declaring that we have the right to be strong and never be afraid. Women (mothers), it is time we stand up and become what God has called us to be.

*I am in Christ, and Satan has no power over me. I overcome evil with good. I am of God and have overcome Satan, for greater is He that is in me than he that is in the world. I will fear no evil for God is with me, His Word and His Spirit comfort me. I am far from oppression and fear does not come near me. No weapon formed against me shall prosper, for my righteousness is of the Lord. Whatever I do will prosper, for I am like a tree that is planted by the rivers of water.*

*I am delivered from the evils of this present world, for it is the will of our God and Father. No evil will befall me, nor shall any plague come near my dwelling, for the Lord has given His angels charge over me, and they keep me in all my ways. In my pathway is life and there is no death. I am a doer of the Word of God and I'm blessed in my deeds. I am happy in things that I do because I am a doer of the Word. (See: 1 Corinthians 12:27; Romans 12:21; Isaiah 54:14; 1 John 4:4; Psalm 23:4 Isaiah 54:17 Galatians 1:4.)*

*Fear, in the name of Jesus I renounce you and tell you that I no longer give place to you in my life. I lay an ax to your root in my life and rip you up and cast you into the pit. I sever any generational curse of fear that could have come to me from my ancestors and I sever any curse of fear from my children or future children. I will no longer be afraid because I have overcome you by the blood of the Lamb. I call forth the gift of faith in my life. Holy Spirit, I ask that You fill me up to overflowing with the love and power of Jesus Christ, the Anointed. In Jesus' name, amen.*

## Taking Faith Action

Take the time to look up these "fear not" scriptures. Ask the Holy Spirit to show you clearly what God promises us when we "fear not." Remember, God is an "if, then" God. *If* you "fear not," *then* God will....

The first three scriptures below are examples of how to find the "if, then" promises for you. After the first three, you write them out too!

| | |
|---|---|
| Genesis 15:1 AMP: | **Fear not, Abram, I am your Shield, your abundant compensation, and your reward shall be exceedingly great.** |
| If/Then Promise: | *If* you *fear not, then* God will be your shield, your abundant compensation, and your great reward! |
| Genesis 21:17 AMP: | **Fear not, for God has heard the voice of the youth where he is.** |
| If/Then Promise: | *If* you *fear not, then* God will hear you and your children! |
| 1 Chronicles 28:20 AMP: | **Fear not, be not dismayed, for the Lord God, my God, is with you. He will not fail or forsake you until you have finished all the work for the service of the house of the Lord.** |

If/Then Promise:      *If* you *fear not, then* God will be
                      with you.  He will not fail or
                      forsake you!

Now continue looking up the rest of scriptures.  Write them out and then write out the "if, then" promise for you!

2 Chronicles 20:17

Genesis 43:23

Exodus 14:13

Exodus 20:20

Deuteronomy 1:21 & Genesis 46:3

Joshua 10:8 & Numbers 21:34

Deuteronomy 20: 3 & 4

Deuteronomy 31:6

Judges 6:23 & Psalm 118:17

Ruth 3:11

2 Kings 6:16

Isaiah 41:10 & Isaiah 41:13

Isaiah 43:1

Isaiah 44:2-4

Luke 8:50

1 John 4:18

# 26
# Proactive Power To Be Free From Fear

And he shall say to them, "Hear, O Israel: Today you are on the verge of battle with your enemies. Do not let your heart faint, *do not be afraid*, and do not tremble or be terrified because of them; for the Lord your God is He who goes with you, to fight for you against your enemies, to save you."

Deuteronomy 20:3-4

Understanding what fear is will help us to walk in victory over it. Fear is actually twisted or perverted faith. Fear is Satan's "faith" in evil. For example, if you fear a big dog, you are putting faith in that dog's ability to hurt you. That is why it is so important that we do not allow ourselves to operate in fear. Fear and faith cannot reside in the same place. Picture it this way, you have a coin and fear is on one side and faith on the other. You are either operating in fear *or* in faith. And the Word of God says that without faith it is impossible to please God (Hebrews 11:6.) Therefore, we must walk in faith instead of fear!

Overcoming fear can sometimes be a process. It can take time to walk out your deliverance. We have a precious young lady named Tracey, who is living with us while she is going to college. She is helping us with the house and the children (not to mention so many other things!). Tracey is like family and we love her dearly.

When Tracey first came to live with us, she began to be attacked by the spirit of fear. She told us she had wrestled with anxiety and fear attacks since she was a tiny child. She would literally spend hours at night praying in the Spirit, binding and rebuking the devil, and basically doing all out combat against fear. She would be awakened, caught off guard, and unable to control the vain imaginations and thoughts that would bombard her.

We stood with her, prayed with her, spoke the Word of God over her, and fought with her for deliverance in this battle. Yet, it seemed she just couldn't get complete victory.

After studying and meditating on scriptures pertaining to fear, the Holy Spirit gave Tracey another tactic against this enemy. She took the Word of God, highlighted a verse she decided to stand on, and left her Bible open to that verse on her night stand. She strategized so she would not be caught off guard in the night hours again. She knew right where her Bible was and exactly what promise from God's Word she was going to use to resist Satan. She predetermined she would immediately take captive whatever fear thought came (it starts with a thought!) and command it to be obedient to Christ (2 Corinthians 10:5). She would immediately pick up the sword of the Spirit (the Word of God) and point out her highlighted scripture to the spirit that was tormenting her. *No more* would the devil build a stronghold of fear in her life.

All the strongholds had been torn down, the spirit of fear had been cast out, and now she was going to be proactive in keeping herself from being in a vulnerable position to fear. By proactive, I mean she was going on the offensive. Once Tracey chose to offensively (instead of defensively) use her "sword" against the spirit of fear, the devil tucked his tail and ran. She no longer had those battles with fear. Later on, after she relaxed and became comfortable again, Satan tried to come back with the same tactic. But Tracey had already discovered how to defeat him, so she went back and started the offensive faith attack with the Word all over again! Fight until you win! Don't quit.

The devil uses such deception with the spirit of fear. I often tell people, if we saw what the devil sees, *we* wouldn't be afraid. Satan is the one who is afraid. He *knows* he is defeated, and he sees the powerful angels of the Lord in the spirit realm. Satan sees the size of our spirit man when we are in Christ — and we are much bigger in the spirit than we are in the natural if we are feeding our spirit man the Word of God!

We can be free from fear. Like Tracey, part of our problem with overcoming this enemy is that we are always *reacting* to fear instead of taking action prior to being attacked. It is vital to ask the Holy Spirit for a strategy through the Word of God *before* Satan hits us with a myriad of thoughts that overwhelm us. We must deal with any strongholds of fear we may currently have, take our fear (the enemy) and beat it as fine as the dust before the wind and cast it out like dirt in the streets as the psalmist says in Psalm 18:42. We need to sever any generational curses of fear in our lives and then take a proactive approach.

The Father God took care of your fear 2000 years ago when He sent Jesus to die on the cross. After Jesus was resurrected, the *first words* He spoke to Mary Magdalene and Mary (*who were women!*) were, **Rejoice! *Do not be afraid.* Go and tell My brethren to go to Galilee, and there they will see Me** (Matthew 28:9-10). Take your fear, lay it at Jesus' feet and *rejoice!* (You can't rejoice and be in fear at the same time!) Go to "Galilee" and put your eyes on Jesus. Then no devil in hell can make you afraid.

## Praying With Power

*Jesus, I thank You that You came, died, and rose again so that You could give me a spirit of power and not of fear (2 Timothy 1:7). I receive Your words in Matthew 28:9-10 and fix my eyes on You. I rejoice that You have conquered fear for me. I choose to walk in faith and inherit the promises that You have for me. Satan, I give you notice that your lies have been revealed and I choose not to fear. Holy Spirit, I thank You that You will help me strategize to be proactive in my stand against the spirit of fear. Thank You Father God, that where Your Spirit is there is freedom. In Jesus' name, amen.*

## Taking Faith Action

Make a list of fears that you may have been dealing with over the past few months (or even years). Ask the Holy Spirit to guide you in uncovering any hidden fears from which you need to be delivered. Remember that there may be a "layer by layer peeling process" that is necessary to uncover a root fear. Yield to the Holy Spirit and be willing to face whatever fears you may have. The Father God will be faithful and not forsake you.

After you have made a list, take the list and write across the top, *"Rejoice! I will not be afraid!"* Also, write 2 Timothy 1:7 out at the bottom of the page and make sure you have it memorized. Now ask the Holy Spirit to guide you as you proactively design a practical plan from God's Word for any attack from the spirit of fear.

# 27

# Soaring Eagles

## by Sharon Daugherty

**But they that wait upon the Lord shall renew their strength; they shall mount up with wings as eagles; they shall run, and not be weary; and they shall walk, and not faint.**

Isaiah 40:31 (KJV)

If there is one thing I have learned through the years in ministry, it is that I must have time alone with God and put His Word in my mind and heart on a daily basis. This is not just to know what to minister to others, but it is for myself — to keep me on the right track. Life seems to get busier, but the peace of God which comes from spending time with Him and meditating in His Word cannot be forfeited. Isaiah 26:3 (KJV) says, **Thou wilt keep him** (or her) **in perfect peace, whose mind is stayed on thee: because he** (or she) **trusteth in thee.**

To wait upon the Lord means to stop and listen to Him. Our minds tell us continually that we have so much to do and so little time to do it. *Stop!* Realize the enemy is subtle and knows if he can keep you from that time, he can keep you from rightly discerning situations and cause you to make decisions or react to others in ways you will later regret.

There is a way to soar above our problems, trials, or testings, to overcome and get a higher view of things so we can properly judge them. That is through time with the Lord, which causes us to hear His voice more clearly and quickly.

Some time ago, my husband preached a message on the topic, "Soaring With Eagles." John was eight years old and

113

Paul was seven years old at the time. After hearing their father's sermon on Sunday, they left for a week of church day camp the following day.

The first day the children were divided into small groups and the counselor asked John and Paul's group, "What name do you want to call yourselves?" Many hands went up. One boy replied *Soaring Eagles*. Obviously, he too had heard the sermon the day before. All of the boys agreed that *Soaring Eagles* would be their name.

The counselor then asked, "Can anyone tell me, What is a soaring eagle?" No one raised their hand except for our son, John. In his eight-year-old mind, he came up with a slightly different interpretation of our being like soaring eagles. He replied, "Miss Daisy! Miss Daisy! I know, I know! It's this really *big* eagle that takes off from the ground, flapping his gigantic wings faster and faster, going higher and higher, and screaming at the top of his lungs because he's got 'sores' all over his body (instead of he "soars" high in the sky)."

The counselor said she had to turn her head to get her composure. When we were told, we had a good laugh too. We obviously had to explain again the biblical meaning of a *soaring eagle* to our son!

Right now you may feel just like John's interpretation of the eagle — flapping your wings as fast as you can, struggling in the flesh, with sores all over your body from wounds accumulated from other people, and screaming at the top of your lungs, "*help!*"

It's time to come apart before you come apart! (Mark 6:31.) Take time with God daily, and you will find, like the eagle, you will rise up from that place. Instead of flapping your wings and struggling underneath the circumstances, you'll catch the wind of God's Spirit and His power will carry you high above, causing you to soar as an overcomer in this life. It's not by your might, nor by your power (fleshly efforts) that you overcome, but it is by His Spirit (Zechariah 4:6). Now you will be able to help others rise above and overcome in His strength.

We are living in evil days in which the enemy is trying to subdue believers, but Jesus has given us the keys to rise and soar as an eagle above the pressures of life.

*Sharon Daugherty is actively involved with her husband, Billy Joe Daugherty, in pastoring at Victory Christian Center in Tulsa, Oklahoma, and raising four children. Both graduates of Oral Roberts University, they travel and minister together throughout the United States and in foreign countries. Sharon is not only a busy mother, but a psalmist, author, and teacher of the Word of God.*

# 28

# Mommy and Daddy
# Love Each Other!

**Beloved, let us love one another: for love is of God; and every one that loveth is born of God, and knoweth God. He that loveth not knoweth not God; for God is love.**

**1 John 4:7-8 (KJV)**

The most important thing we can do for our children is for mommy and daddy to love each other. Harry and I spend so much time teaching our children to love each other. We are always telling them, "Don't fight or argue with each other. This is the only brother you have on this earth. Learn how to get along with each other. Take care of your sister. Watch over and defend each other."

Our children do these things willingly because they have been taught (repeatedly) that this is the way to show love for one another. Yet there is one way Harry and I have found that is much more effective! Let *your* love for one another (you and your spouse) be clearly evident in all you do and say! Children do what they see. Children say what they hear. If children badger, bicker, and belittle one another, take a look at your marriage relationship. Are you doing the same thing?

Harry and I love each other very much and have just recently fallen in love with each other all over again! It has been so good for our children. In the process of ten years and three children, we got a little too busy to spend that extra moment to be affectionate with one another. Now I'm not saying we were not affectionate at all, but I am saying it was not a constant natural response in our home. Our

117

children need that, and we didn't even know we were not doing it until we started doing it again!

Now Harry and I are automatically kissing each other and holding each other, and I am always sitting on "Daddy's" lap. We hold hands almost constantly — in the car, walking — anywhere! It is definitely wonderful for us, but I think it is even more wonderful for our children. Lil' Harry, Roman, and Gabrielle are seeing that affection is an outward sign of an inward feeling Harry and I have for each other.

You see, we have always been affectionate toward our children — constantly loving on them and reaffirming them as special and valuable. This is very important to do. However, it needs to be backed up with actions in the parent relationship also. You might be thinking, "Well, I can't do it all by myself and my mate is totally cold to me unless sex is involved." Don't be discouraged. You can make a difference. Start on your side.

Watch what you say to (and about) your mate at all times, but especially in front of your children. Say loving, kind, responsive, and uplifting things to your mate. Do things that are unexpected for your partner and watch the sparks begin to fly again. Don't just try it for a few days and get discouraged. Stay with it — it works!

You may be able to share some of what you are doing with your mate or you might be better off to keep it all to yourself and just show him with your actions. People respond to being loved and cared for and esteemed higher than yourself. The response will come. Just don't get disheartened and quit. Stay with it until the desired result is achieved. This action between you and your mate helps set the tone in the home. Once the affectionate tone is set, then the children will automatically do and say what they have seen and heard.

God shows up in our lives when we act like Him. He doesn't when we don't! When your children get so accustomed to the peace of God resting on your home, they will help you to create the same atmosphere.

Sometimes when Harry and I are talking to each other about something that happened during the day, our voices will raise in telling the story. Lil' Harry will get so upset if he thinks one of us is being negative to the other and he will say, "Daddy (or Mommy), don't talk to my mommy (or daddy) that way!" This has been a great lesson for us. Even though we were not talking ugly to one another, it has taught us that the children are always listening even when we think they are not! And it hurts their spirits (and their self-confidence, self-worth, and comfort zone) if they think that something is not in harmony in their world.

It is up to us to teach our children how to respond to one another. If we parents criticize each other, so will our children. If we are impatient with each other, then so are they. If we are unloving to each other, then so are they. If we are frustrated with each other and do a bunch of yelling or mumbling under our breath, then so will they. Whatever we do, they will do!

Having children puts a lot of pressure on us to be more like Jesus. Isn't that something? Our children constantly help our walk with the Lord by being a "watch dog" on our tongues and actions for us! Let's use this to our advantage and start correcting our daily actions and words.

You will be amazed how your home, your children, your marriage, your attitude, and everything about your life will improve. And someday your child's spouse will thank you — because *your* child will love *their* mate the way they see *you* love *yours.*

## Praying With Power

*Thank You, God, for being a loving Father to me. Thank You that You are love, and that Your love flows through us so that we*

119

can love one another. Thank You that You are an affectionate God (Philippians 1:8). Father God, I ask that You make my spouse and me more aware of our example of Your love to our children.

I pray that You will rekindle (or expand) that beautiful, unconditional, affectionate love from You between my beloved and me. Give us the ability to watch our words and actions with diligence. Help us to speak loving, kind, edifying words to one another. Help us to do even the little things that show our inward love for each other. Thank You that our children will receive in their minds and spirits this example of Your love. I pray that they will also pass this on to their spouse and their children. In Jesus' name, amen.

*A note to the single parent:* Pray this same prayer over yourself and your children. Ask for the extra measure of grace needed for being a single parent. Know that the Father God will meet you in your need. You can practice the love talk by talking out loud to the Father God. Peace is set in the home by the parent and your children will follow what they see and hear!

## Taking Faith Action

Take the time today to write your spouse a note telling him how much you love him. (If you are a single parent, you can write to the Father God.) Tell him how much you thank God that He put you together as parents for your children. Pray about talking to your mate regarding ways you can create a more affectionate atmosphere in your home. Follow the Holy Spirit's lead and take steps toward expressing the God-given affection for your husband. Take the time to tell your children how much you love their "Daddy."

# 29

# Father of the Fatherless
## by Patricia White (Harry's Mother)

I had been happily married for sixteen years when my life began to change drastically. On my sixteenth wedding anniversay, June 1, 1968, my precious husband, Harry Salem, was diagnosed with leukemia, and on November 9, 1968, only five months and nine days later, he went home to be with the Lord.

I was left with three children, ages ten, thirteen, and fifteen, to rear by myself. I went to my mother's home for about a week following the funeral and then returned to our home to try and begin living again without my dear husband.

In trying to return to the routine of things, I began to realize that I just couldn't do this by myself. Even though Harry had been a very busy man with his work and even the past months with his illness, he was still there to back me up in my decisions, physically and emotionally. Now there was no one to help me, no one to reassure me that I was making the correct choices for my young children whose futures were now entirely in my hands.

I was lying on the couch one night (I just couldn't make myself sleep in our bed alone) and I began to feel an uncontrollable emotion of being overwhelmed by the responsibility of it all. I began to talk to my Father and spill out my heart's anguish and fears of the future. I told God, "I don't think I can do this, Father."

As I lay there, the Holy Spirit began to take me back in my memory to a time when I was a little girl and I was talking to my grandfather Orme. We were discussing the matter of orphan children, and I was very concerned about their well-being and who would take care of them since they had no daddy or mother. My grandfather, who loved God with all his heart, told me that the Bible says God will be a Father to the orphan and a husband to the widow (Psalm 68:5, 146:9, and Deuteronomy 10:18). I didn't even know what a widow was at that time in my life, but when that memory came flooding ack to me lying on that couch, it brought such peace and assurance to my heart that I was not alone personally nor as a parent!

When I remembered the words of my grandfather quoting the Bible to me, being the nature I am and having the relationship that I have with the Father, I immediately believed God's Word to be true and peace beyond my own comprehension flooded my very being.

We got through the next few months, the teenage years, and the college years knowing that God was watching over us and protecting us and providing for us. There were times when things would happen and I would not know what to do. I would just go to my husband, the Father, and I would say, "Your children are not behaving and I have done all I know to do and it's not working. I think You are going to have to correct them." And you know what? He always did, just like a natural father.

Over the years things have not always been easy, but I know the Father God watches over His Word to perform it (Isaiah 55:11, Ezekiel 12:25). He has proven to me over and over again that He truly will be a Father to the orphan and a husband to the widow. All three of my children are now grown and serving God. I could not ask for a better husband than the Father. He truly is Father to my children and a husband to this widow!

*Patrician Christensen Salem White is a woman of faith. She is the mother of three children (Stephanie Cantees, Lindsay Roberts, and Harry Salem II), grandmother of ten, and great-grandmother of one. Patricia says, "The greatest quality you can pass on to all children is that all the promises in God's Word are true and that they can and will be theirs if they will only trust and believe Him." She is called as an intercessory prayer warrior and takes her calling very seriously.*

# 30
# Putting "Control" on the Altar

*Have you not known? Have you not heard? Has it not been told you from the beginning? Have you not understood from the foundations of the earth? It is He who sits above the circle of the earth, and its inhabitants are like grasshoppers, Who stretches out the heavens like a curtain, and spreads them out like a tent to dwell in.*

**Isaiah 40:21-22**

Read Isaiah 40:12-31 and remind yourself just who it is that really is in control! So many times we parents feel completely out of control. That feeling seems to go right along with the learning process in parenting! Ha! *It sure is tough to not be in control!*

When Gabrielle was born and had sleep apnea, I developed a habit of getting up with her every time she cried. As the months progressed this became a terrible problem. Sometimes she would get up as many as twenty-five times a night! It came to the point where I was either not sleeping at all or only a few minutes at a time when I did get to sleep.

I became very ill in my body and my emotions. I lost my voice completely (for almost a year!) and was beginning to feel completely hopeless and out of control of my life. I knew that my only hope was to get some quality rest for an extended period of time. That meant taking charge of Gabrielle's sleep problem, which had become my sleep problem! I knew what to do, but wanted reassurance. Since she had suffered with the sleep apnea, I think subconsciously she was afraid to get too deeply asleep — thus the cries for "Mama" all night long.

I found a leading children's book on sleep problems and promptly scanned the problems discussed to find those similar to Gabrielle's condition. It only took a few minutes to locate the desired result needed for proper rest for both of us and the method needed to obtain it. The problem was I had unknowingly trained Gabrielle to go to sleep sucking on something, and when she awakened in the night the only way she knew to go back to sleep was to have her familiar sucking object in her mouth. Unless I got up and retrieved the thing and put it back in her mouth, there was no sleep to be had. This was because she had been trained to fall asleep this way.

The book made it plain that a retraining process was necessary to obtain proper rest for all concerned. This meant several nights and days (during nap time) of hours of constant crying. Even though this was an extremely painful process, I stuck right with the plan and it only took three days and nights to retrain Gabrielle to a new method of falling asleep.

Now we go to bed at the same time each night (if at all possible) with a nightly routine of kissing all the family, sitting in the rocking chair, singing a few songs, saying our prayers, and having a few minutes of conversation. Then I ask her if she is ready to get into her bed and go to sleep. She almost always leans forward and says yes. If on occasion she says no, I wait a few minutes, we sing or talk a few minutes more and then I ask her again. She is usually ready by then.

I take her to bed with her favorite animals and "babies." I kiss her, tell her I love her, and tell her good night as I leave the room. (Or Harry may do the honors.) It usually takes less than five minutes for her to go to sleep. If she wakes up in the night, she goes back to sleep on her own, because she has been taught to go to sleep without any stimulus and without having anyone with her. Praise God!

(I know *many* of you can relate to this, *Praise God!*) I now get plenty of sleep and my health and my voice are returning!

It sounds so simple, doesn't it? We took control of our daughter instead of her taking control of us. As I was rocking and loving on Gabrielle one night, I said to her, "It sure is tough not to be in control, isn't it?" You know what the Father God said to me? "It sure is Cheryl, isn't it?"

You see, just like I (as the parent) wanted Gabrielle to get on a good schedule of rest, not just for me but for her little body, the Father God wants to have control of our lives for our benefit. He desires to help us, but God can only do that when we give up control and allow Him full charge over our lives and our futures.

For some personalities, giving up control is so easy — trusting someone else to take care of everything. However, for some of our personalities (mine included) giving up control and allowing God to have full reign is so difficult! Yet it is not impossible. It just takes training, like we had to do with Gabrielle's sleep problem. It may take a few nights and days, (or weeks and months!) to finally be comfortable with the Father being in full charge of everything. But it is so worth it! When the Father God is in control, we receive the full benefit of all He has for us.

Make a conscious effort to "give it all up." Make an altar in your home if you do not already have one, a place where you can go daily to take "control" and give it to the Lord. You will find that eventually it will stay on the altar. Life is so much easier and so much sweeter when we give the Father God complete control of our lives.

## Praying With Power

*Father, I worship You for being the Most High God Who is omnipotently and omnisciently in control of heaven and earth. Thank You that You want to be so intricately involved in my personal life that You want to be in charge of even the smallest details. Thank You that You are a good God and have my best interest at heart; therefore, I can trust You to be in control of all of my life — including my children. I ask that You give me wisdom in not allowing my children to control me, so they will understand from childhood that You are in charge. Lord Jesus, I lay "control" on the altar and ask that You give me courage to trust You. Father God, I give You full reign of my life. In Jesus' name, amen.*

## Taking Faith Action

List three areas where you feel you must be in "control":

(1)

(2)

(3)

Picture yourself literally taking these three areas and laying each one on the altar. If you have a designated "altar" in your home, take something that symbolizes that particular area and "give it up to the Lord" on the altar. Ask the Holy Spirit to enlighten you as to the root cause of your need to be in control. Is there a root of fear? Is there a root of rejection? Let the Holy Spirit help you deal with the spirit of control and bring you to the liberty of letting the Father be in charge.

# 31
# Teaching Responsibility
## by Peggy Capps

So then, each of us will give an account of himself to God.

**Romans 14:12 (NIV)**

It is very important to let a child learn responsibility for his own decisions. I'll never forget one Wednesday night when we were getting ready to go to church. Our daughter, Beverly, wanted to stay home. She began to come up with all kinds of excuses like, "I have a lot of homework," etc. My husband, Charles, looked at her for a minute and then said, "Beverly, I will leave that decision up to you. You just do what you think will be the best thing to do."

Beverly looked at her dad and said, "Oh, Daddy that's not fair." You see, she wanted him to tell her it would be all right to stay at home so he would be the one to blame and not her.

She decided to go to church that night.

# 32

# Do *You* Need Rest?

**My Presence will go with you, and I will give you rest.**

Exodus 33:14

Jesus was not "need" led, He was "Spirit" led. We, as God's women, need to follow His example. The devil has literally run us women ragged, trying to meet all the needs of all the people. In the process, *we have forgotten to spend time with Jesus.*

The Father God says in Isaiah 30:15 (AMP), "In returning [to Me] and resting [in Me] you shall be saved; in quietness and in [trusting] confidence shall be your strength." Have you come to the point lately where you just cannot find any strength? You have so much to do that you just don't have enough strength to do it all? The way to get your strength back is by returning to the Father and resting in Him.

How many of you feel like you could really use a rest? Most every woman I know could use a rest. Yet *how* to *get rest* seems to be the real problem. You know you *need* rest, but *how* do you get it? You have *so much* you have to do — it is not even a matter of *"need* to do" anymore, it is *"have* to do," isn't it?

Women are busy, busy, busy. I know they are. I am one. And I am busy, busy, busy. An old Chinese proverb says, "Man who says it can't be done shouldn't interrupt woman who is doing it!" I love that. There is some truth in that. Ha! Yet a woman's busyness can be used against her.

When we as women get too busy, Satan can use that against us to steal our fellowship time with the Father. Remember, the Father *deserves* our time, but we *need* that time. I think in the 90's we think that "Blessed are the busy" is a new beatitude! Well, that is not the truth! We *need* rest and the Father *wants* us to rest! In fact, in Matthew 11:28 God beckons, Come unto me and I will give you rest. Running *away* from your problems is not finding your rest. Hiding for a weekend is not finding your rest. You are only going to find your rest by running to the Father. He wants us to come to Him and let *Him* give us rest. And we find that rest in His presence.

God deserves, and we need, a quiet time set aside for Him — a time to be alone with Him. We say, "I don't have that time. I would love to have that time." Well, Matthew 6:33 says that if we will seek *first* the kingdom of God, all things will be added to us.

How often do you hear people, especially women, say things like: "I would do so-and-so if I just had the time. I would exercise if I just had the time. I would eat right if I just had the time. I would spend time with the Lord if I just had the time." Time is something that we can reap from the Father, *after* we plant the *seed of time*.

If you are a person who just never has enough time, then maybe you are not planting enough time with the Father to reap a harvest. If at the end of your day there is more work left than there is time to finish up that work, then not enough "time seed" has been planted with the Father.

And one thing women don't have enough of *is* time. If you don't plant time, you'll *never* have enough time. However, if you plant time with the Father God, *somehow* He grows your time. It is the same principle of reaping what you sow that works in other areas such as finances (Galatians 5:7).

God will increase your time so that you can accomplish what you are called to accomplish. The Father will multiply your time so you can get done everything that you *have* to get done. You will have the time needed and you will not even know how! When you plant your time, God will be faithful to increase it. With the demand on women today, we need that increase!

It seems in this day and age women have to be "professionals" at everything, even in our own homes! We have to become "professional" mothers, doctors, teachers, household engineers, plumbers, electricians, auto-mechanics, organizers of every function (from home, office, or business), luncheons, parties, school functions (of every variety), accountants, financial wizards (with a small budget of course), gourmet chefs, chauffeurs, seamstresses, cleaners (from household to laundry), and when all else is finished — don't forget that you have to be a *professional lover* at the end of the day!!! We have to be *all things* to *all* people. These are just the *minimum* requirements for women in today's society.

Mamas, listen to me. Don't get so busy doing what you are called to do that your children suffer. If I came to a point in my life where our children were grown and they hated the ministry because they lost their mama (time wise) because of it — anything else that I may have "done" for the Father would not be worth anything. Give your time to your children — *they are worth it*!

So where do we find the time to spend quality time with the Father? Remember, we do not *have* time to pray and grow. We have to *make* time to pray and grow. There is a difference. If you look to *have time* to pray and grow, you will never have it. You must *make time* — you *set aside time* to pray and grow.

Satan does not want you to become spiritually knowledgeable and quit being spiritually ignorant. Therefore, he does not want you to have time to pray and grow — because then you will know how to beat him up, defeat him, and stomp all over his head!

I want to tell you a story of a little girl who was learning to ride her bike. Her daddy was helping her and she had mastered riding her bike in the back yard, the front yard, and the driveway. Now she was ready to tackle the big hill out back. Her daddy took her to the top of the hill and helped her get set for the big moment. He went halfway down the hill to be a source of encouragement, and the last thing he said to her was, "Remember the most important lesson I taught you!" The little girl hollered back, "Okay, Daddy, I got it!" And she was off!

As she flew past her daddy with a panicked look on her face, he realized she had forgotten the most important lesson he had taught her. "Daddy, I forgot how to stop!!" she screamed. She got to the bottom of the hill and crashed.

The Father wants us to remember how to stop. It is such an important lesson for us that God emphasized the point by taking a whole day of rest (on the seventh day) when He created the world. *God* didn't need to rest! He needed *us* to know (and He showed us by example) that *we need* to stop and rest.

Take a day and say no to work and yes to resting in the Father. Give God your time. If God doesn't have your time, He really doesn't have you. Go ahead, relax in the Father's presence, take time in His glory. And remember, the Father God *deserves* for us to stop, rest, and give Him our time, but we *need* it. He *deserves* it, we *need* it!

## Praying With Power

*Jesus, I thank You that You have said if I will come to You, You will give me rest. I thank You that You are the Peace-speaker, and when You speak You bring calmness and rest. Father, I claim Your Word in Galatians 6:7 and I commit to You to sow seeds of time, knowing that You will bring a harvest that will enable me to accomplish all that You have called me to do. I call forth increase into my life and thank You, Father, for increasing my time. I choose to* **make time** *for being in Your wonderful presence. I ask You, Holy Spirit, to help me keep my time for my husband and children of utmost priority. Help me not to get so busy trying to reach the destination that I miss the blessings of the journey. I give You the honor and glory for loving me enough to be my refuge and my place of rest. In Jesus' name, amen.*

## Taking Faith Action

1. Look up these *rest* scriptures. List the benefits of *rest:* Deuteronomy 12:9; Psalm 16:9; Proverbs 19:23; Isaiah 32:18; Jeremiah 6:16; Hebrews 4:9-11; Matthew 11:28-29.

2. Pray about tithing your time. There are 168 hours in a week. Tithe 16.8 hours (10 percent) of your time to the Father God!

# 33

# When God Says, "Pssst"!

## by Gloria Copeland

**For the Lord is good; His mercy is everlasting, and his truth endures to all generations.**

**Psalm 100:5**

Did you know your children are in your heart? It's true! You carry your children in your heart the same way God carries you in His heart.

You can feel what's going on with them even when they're on the other side of the world. If they're hurt, if they're lonely, or if they're toying with sin and getting off track — when things are wrong or things are right — you can feel it.

I remember when Ken and I were in Australia once. We were flying from one city to another and suddenly thoughts of our son John flooded my heart. John was a teenager at the time and he was all boy. He rode everything with wheels — cars, trucks, motorcycles, dune buggies — and it seemed he was always turning something over.

That day on the plane, I was concerned about him. I knew how much the devil would like to sneak in and steal his life, and I was concerned that John's misadventures could give the devil the opportunity to do it. But the Holy Spirit broke in on my thoughts. He spoke to Ken and said, "My mercy hovers over John." When Ken relayed those words to me, all my fears vanished.

"My mercy hovers over John." I'll never forget that promise! As I've prayed for John throughout the years, that wonderful word from God would often rise up and remind me that John's life was secure. It would assure me that God would keep him and hold him steady until the day he got things straight in his life.

"My mercy hovers over your child." That is a wonderful word from God for you too. If God will do that for my child, He will do it for yours. The covenant God has made with you in the blood of Jesus extends to your children and your children's children. Psalm 103:17 (KJV) says, **But the mercy of the Lord is from everlasting to everlasting upon them that fear him, and his righteousness unto children's children.**

Our children and grandchildren are covered in our covenant with God. Everything God gives to me, He'll give to them. All the protection that I have, He passes on to my family.

If you are a believer and you're willing to trust God for the deliverance and salvation of your children, you will not be disappointed.

*Gloria Copeland is an author, teacher, and ordained minister. She and her husband, Kenneth (founder of Kenneth Copeland Ministries), minister through television, the printed page, teaching tapes, meetings, and conventions worldwide. For years now, Gloria's love of people has stirred her to share with thousands, both lost and saved, how the Word of God, as revealed in Jesus Christ, has taken her from a life of failure and defeat to a life of thrilling victory.*

# 34

# "And a Child Shall Lead Them"

**Josiah was *eight years old* when he became king, and he reigned thirty-one years in Jerusalem. His mother's name was Jedidah the daughter of Adaiah of Bozkath.** *And he did what was right in the sight of the Lord, and walked in all the ways of his father David;* **he did not turn aside to the right hand or to the left.**

**2 Kings 22:1-2**

Do we really understand that our children are gifts in the body of Christ and their godly lives will greatly impact nations in these last days? Do we comprehend the call on their generation? I believe the Spirit of God Almighty will be poured out on our sons and daughters in a greater magnitude than ever before!

So often we underestimate the Lord's divinely orchestrated plan and how He will use the *children* to change the world. Josiah became king of Judah when he was eight years old! (2 Kings 22:1.) And the *New King James Version's* commentary of that verse says that Judah was *blessed with a last great revival* under Josiah's rule!

We must get into our spirits that *our* children will rule and reign through Jesus Christ in this "last great revival" God is pouring out upon the earth! We must prepare our children to fulfill what He has called them to do.

Second Kings 22:2 says that Josiah **did what was right in the sight of the Lord, and walked in all the ways of his** *father* **David; he did not turn aside to the right hand or to the left.** David's walk with the Lord impacted Josiah three hundred years later, and Josiah chose to do what was right and never turned aside to the right or to the left. Josiah reigned for thirty-one years! That is quite a track record of not messing up! David taught God's ways to his lineage and they prevailed in Josiah's life. We are to put the things of God into our children.

Several years ago I was emceeing the Miss Oklahoma Pageant and Lil' Harry and Roman wanted to come up on the stage. We agreed that they could come up during a commercial break with their little tuxedos on, for just a brief moment. I told them it would have to be quick and they wouldn't be able to say anything. When the time came, our handsome little guys came up there and in front of thousands of people Lil' Harry says, "Mom, I have something to say." What was I to do? So I said, "Make it quick, son".

Five year old Lil' Harry took the microphone and laid out the plan of salvation before the entire crowd at the Miss Oklahoma Pageant. Needless to say, I was stunned. I was praying, "Oh God, Oh God." When he finished, the crowd gave him a standing ovation for sharing the plan of salvation! Afterwards, a woman met me in the bathroom and said, "If there was anyone in there that didn't receive Jesus, it wasn't because their heart wasn't touched."

When we parents put the Word and ways of God in them, it will come out! The Word of God will come out of our children right when the Father God wants it to come out of them. What a privilege and responsibility we have to train our children in the ways of the Father God. Yet, we see the joy set before them in knowing that God's Spirit will lead them and pour on and through them in these last days.

And it shall come to pass afterward that I will pour out My Spirit on all flesh; your sons and your daughters shall prophesy, your old men shall dream dreams, your young men shall see visions. And also on My menservants and on My maidservants I will pour out My

Spirit in those days. And I will show wonders in the heavens and in the earth: blood and fire and pillars of smoke. The sun shall be turned into darkness, and the moon into blood, before the coming of the great and awesome day of the Lord. And it shall come to pass that whoever calls on the name of the Lord shall be saved.

**Joel 2:28-32**

As Christians, *our children* really are the future. They are the ones God will use to lead their generation to Jesus as Lord and Savior. *Our children* shall be a part of those who announce Jesus' return and proclaim with urgency, "The King is coming!" *Our children* will help create the atmosphere for God's glory to consume the earth. *Our children* will be astride those beautiful white horses alongside the King of kings and Lord of lords when He makes His triumphant return! (Revelation 19:11-16.) What a glorious privilege we have to be their parents — to impart into their spirits and lead them by our godly example. Oh, parents, hear me! We are the parents of a special generation of believers. The Father God trusted us enough to give us these little "kings and priests of the Lord" to train for Him.

Catch the vision that the Father has for your anointed little ones. Speak to them the greatness that God has for their lives in changing their generation. Put the Word of God into their hearts and call forth the anointing of the Holy Spirit upon them. Then watch the Heavenly Father use your children to lead the lost to Him.

The wolf also shall dwell with the lamb, the leopard shall lie down with the young goat, the calf and the young lion and the fatling together; *and a little child shall lead them.*

**Isaiah 11:6**

## Praying With Power

*Jesus — King of kings and Lord of lords — I exalt You high above the heavens and the earth. I lift You up in honor and adoration. I magnify Your Holy Name. No One is holy like You, Lord, for there is none beside You. My heart rejoices in You, Oh God. Father, like Hannah prayed for Samuel (1 Samuel 1:27-28), I pray from my heart, "For this child I prayed, and You granted me my petition which I asked of You. Therefore, I also give _____ to You — as long as he/she lives.*

*Father, I call my children (and my future children) and the children in this world out of darkness and into light. I claim Your Word that says we (and my children) are "a chosen generation, a royal priesthood, a holy nation, Your own special people, that we may proclaim the praises of You Who called me out of darkness into light." (1 Peter 2:9.)*

*Thank You, Father, that I am Yours and You will pour out Your Spirit on my sons and daughters in these last days, and that they will make a difference for You. Give me wisdom, Lord, to train and impart into my children all that You have ordained for me to put into them as their parent. I'm grateful for this privilege. In the mighty name of Jesus, amen.*

## Taking Faith Action

Have you caught God's vision for your children? Do you see the "king" qualities in them with which God could rule a nation? Ask the Holy Spirit to reveal to you today God's vision for your children (and this chosen generation of children). Ask the Father to change your perspective from raising your children to one of rearing them to be "kings" (even at eight like Josiah)! In the natural, we can't even fathom an eight-year-old king. However, God has not changed, and if He used a godly eight-year-old boy then, He can surely use an eight-year-old boy today! Ask the Holy Spirit to guide you in ways that you can encourage your children to "operate" in their gifts and callings even at an early age. Remember, they are training to reign with Christ.

# 35

# "Hello, Miss America"

**Let no corrupt word proceed out of your mouth, but what is good for necessary edification, that it may impart grace to the hearers.**

**Ephesians 4:29**

In 1980 I stood on a runway, a crown on my head, roses in my arm, and a banner across my chest that read, "Miss America." God told me I would be Miss America, and I had worked long and hard to achieve the dream God had put in my heart. It all started with a seed God planted. Was it a supernatural dream? Did God tell me in a booming voice? No, God started the whole thing with a milkman.

Our family was very poor and my finest dresses were made of flour sacks! So when the milkman would come to deliver our milk, there I was, quite dowdy I suppose. Yet every week I would come to the door and the milkman would greet me with, "Hello, Miss America." He would continue and tell me that someday *I would be Miss America*. And you know what? I *believed* him.

I believed the words of that milkman so much that it enabled God to fulfill a part of His destiny for my life. And that destiny included *me*, a poor little girl from Choctaw County, Mississippi, being crowned "Miss America 1980."

The words we speak over our children (and others for that matter) are so important. Proverbs 18:21 says **Death and life are in the power of the tongue.** Our words can be the springboard from which the Father God instills and brings life to His divine purpose for our children — or our words can be the quicksand the devil uses to keep our children from fulfilling God's destiny for their lives.

We Christian parents usually don't go around belittling our children or speaking harshly to them. However, do we count the cost of every word that comes out of our mouths? Matthew 12:36-37 warns us, **But I say to you that for every idle word men may speak, they will give account of it in the day of judgment. For by your words you will be justified, and by your words you will be condemned.** We are to watch every word, because the words we speak are so powerful. What about the things we unintentionally say like, "Poor baby," or "Bad boy!" We certainly don't want our children to be poor or bad, so why speak those words over them?

I can hear some of you sighing — like you don't have enough to think about already, right? Well, it is a process of training yourself. It is not as hard as it sounds! Once you get into the mindset and habit of speaking only edifying things over your children, you *can* correct, discipline, and train without negative words. Even more significant are the "life" words that you speak to your children.

Just like the milkman, you have the beautiful privilege of speaking life into someone. You may be the person God uses to plant hope in another's heart. As a parent, our words are to be continually used to cause hope to rise up in our children. The hope we plant in our children will be a blueprint for faith to follow in the years to come. You'll speak the Word of God to your children, hope will rise up within them, and faith will follow right through the door!

Our discouraging words can be detrimental to our children. We must listen to our children's dreams, let them imagine what they might be, and don't discourage their ideas — no matter how ridiculous they might sound to us. We can pour cold water on our children's dreams by a simple word. We must watch our words! We must pray that the Father God will give us the vision of our children the way He sees them. Then we must look past the natural to call those things that are not as though they were. That is what God does:

> God, who gives life to the dead and *calls those things which do not exist as though they did.*
>
> **Romans 4:17**

We are able to love our children unconditionally when we see them the way God sees them. Therefore, we can believe in our children regardless of their behavior (whether good or bad) and speak positively to them and about them.

Even though your precious little darling may be going through a "training phase" with regard to temper tantrums, you can still look at him and say, "You are a mighty man of God!" Pray that the Father God will give you a clarity of purpose and destiny for your child, and then speak it out! For instance, the Holy Spirit has shown me that our little girl has a strong prophetic anointing on her life. Every opportunity I have I say to her, "You are a prophet for the Lord and you are anointed for His glory." With my words, I am speaking life into her and calling forth the anointing on her life.

Ephesians 4:29 in *The Living Bible* says, **Don't use bad language. Say only what is good and helpful to those you are talking to, and what will give them a blessing.** That really sums it up, doesn't it? Every word we speak should be a blessing. And the only way our tongues can be tamed is through the power of the Holy Spirit.

Give the Holy Spirit full reign on your tongue and choose to speak life to your spouse and your children. Your words could change their destiny.

## Praying With Power

*Father, I realize that I have the power of life or death in my tongue. I choose to speak life and submit my tongue to the Holy Spirit. Holy Spirit, I ask You to come alongside me to tame my tongue. I ask that You give me wisdom and diligence in training myself to speak only edifying things to my children and others.*

*Holy Spirit, I ask that You clearly reveal to me the callings and anointings on my children's lives so that I may speak words of life over them and to them in those areas. Thank You, Father, that You have positioned me as a parent to help plant hope within my children. Help me to seize every opportunity to edify my mate and children with my words. I claim Luke 12:12 that says the Holy Spirit will give me the words to say when I need them. In Jesus name, amen.*

## Taking Faith Action

Florence Littauer has written a book entitled, *Silver Boxes*. The book is about encouraging words. In one of her speaking engagements a child responded to her talk about edifying words with the statement, "Our words should be like silver boxes with bows on top!" Not a bad analogy! Our words *should* be like presents!

Make yourself a silver box (or something that will remind you!). Put it where you need to be reminded the most that your words need to be edifying. Soon you'll see that speaking positively will come naturally.

Memorize Ephesians 4:29!

# 36

# Let Your Light Shine

## by Gloria Copeland

**No one after he has lighted a lamp covers it with a vessel or puts it under a couch; but he puts it on a lamp-stand, that those who come in may see the light.**

**Luke 8:16 (AMP)**

Your example will go a lot further than your words. When our son John was a little boy, we were spending time with my grandparents. John was sleeping with my granddaddy and he woke him up in the night and said, "Pop, I have an earache. Would you pray for it?"

Well, my grandparents were raised in a church that didn't believe in healing. I don't know what Pop did, but it didn't work. So, John just got up and said, "I'm going to go get in bed with my mother. When she prays, it stops hurting." About eighteen years later, Pop told me the story.

You see, I had set an example of faith and love and John remembered it. While your children are growing up, they might forget some of the sermons you've preached or act like they're not interested in the things of God. However, they will never forget your *example*.

# 37

# The Purest Praise

**One generation shall praise Your works to another, and shall declare Your mighty acts.**

**Psalm 145:4**

Are you a praiser? Do you love to worship the Father God? I hope so, because your children are watching you. They are recording your actions and feelings about the Father God. And if you praise and worship Him, it will be the natural and normal thing for them to do.

Harry and I love to praise and worship the Lord. I have sung all my life and given God the glory. In fact, my name (Cheryl) means "song of God" in Hebrew. My spirit man overflows with songs of exaltation to the Father God. The passion of my heart is singing and worshipping the Lord. So naturally our children have experienced praise and worship from the womb. By our example and our passion for praise and worship, Harry and I are teaching our children the importance and power of worshipping the Father God. Lil' Harry, Roman, and Gabrielle truly do give God the praise!

The above verse exhorts (and actually commands) us to teach our children to praise God. It is important that we pass the praise of God from generation to generation. We cannot just assume that our children will praise the Lord. We must *teach* them to be praisers! We must teach them by our example and our words. We cannot begin too soon!

Even in the womb our children should constantly be exposed to praise songs and words of adoration to our Father God. Then as little babies, we can sing them songs of praise and worship, and pray over them words of exaltation to the Lord. As our children become toddlers and then adolescents, they are *already* on a *pathway of praise*. The Word says, **Let everything that has breath praise the Lord** (Psalm 150:6). Therefore, from birth we are created and called to praise Him.

Children's praise is so precious. If you want to have your heart touched, just watch as your children praise the Father God. Children are the purest of praisers! They do not have the inhibitions and "religious" hang-ups that many adults have. They just give God their unadulterated love and honor. Their spirits are very sensitive to the Holy Spirit, and they are quick to respond with a heart of praise (if they have been nurtured and taught to praise Him).

One afternoon we were getting ready to leave on a trip. Lil' Harry and I had already situated ourselves in the van while Harry went inside to gather up the luggage. I went back into the house to get something I had forgotten. When I returned to the van I found Lil' Harry in the back seat with tears streaming down his face and his hands lifted in worship as the song, *You Are the Christ* (from one of my albums), was playing.

I wouldn't have dreamed of interrupting Lil' Harry. He was so enthralled in the presence of the Lord! When the song was over and he opened his eyes, I asked him, "Does that song make you sad?" Seven-year-old Lil' Harry replied, "No, Mom, that song just touched me so that I *had to praise* the Lord!" My heart was so moved, and at that moment God gave me a glimpse of what He must feel when He sees His children's hands and hearts lifted in worship.

## Praying With Power

*Father God, the Most High God of all the earth, You are the Creator and Sustainer of all that was, is, and ever will be. I praise You for Your mighty acts, and I praise You according to Your excellent greatness! I WILL extol You, my God and my King, and I will bless Your Name forever and ever. Every day I will bless You and I will praise Your Name.*

*Holy Spirit, I ask that You fill me to overflowing with worship to the Father God. I pray that the love, honor, and adoration in my heart for my King so overwhelms me that I cannot help but cry out in praise and worship. I surrender all of myself in complete devotion to my God. I empty myself so that Your Spirit, Oh God, may consume me and cause me to exalt Your Holy Name.*

*Now Father, I pray that my children may always bless Your Name. I thank You that they are praisers and worshipers of You. I thank You that they will give You glory all the days of their lives. I make the commitment to lead my children by example and teach them by the power of the Holy Spirit to praise You. I thank You that my children shall declare Your mighty works to their generation. I thank You that even my children's children will praise You. In the precious name of Jesus, amen.*

## Taking Faith Action

Look up Psalm 71:14

In this scripture the psalmist is making a commitment to praise God more and more! He is saying he will find new and fresh ways to praise God! We shouldn't abandon our old ways of praise, but we need to become creative in our praise to God! God is creative in meeting our needs — and He loves creativity in our praise!

*Think of several ways that you can be creative in your praise and start praising the Lord in a new way today!*

# 38

# A Willful Choice of the Heart

**And let us not grow weary while doing good, for in due season we shall reap if we do not lose heart.**
**Galatians 6:9**

How many moms (yourself included) do you know who are just plain weary? Unfortunately, the word *"weary"* applies to so many mothers. Whether you are a "stay-at-home mom" or a "corporate mom," all mothers have one thing in common — we can all become weary in our well-doing. Wearing so many different hats as a wife, mother, employee, etc., can cause us to become weary. In fact, many moms today are in bondage to a yoke of weariness.

Weariness can rob us of the joy the Father God wants us to reap in our lives as women of God. God knew this would be a challenge so He addressed this very issue in His Word. I think the Father God put Galatians 6:9 in the Bible just for us moms!

As mothers, we are doing *good* when we give our all to being the best wife, mother, worker, minister, etc. that we can possibly be. However, when we get into such exhaustion that our health (physically, emotionally, or spiritually) suffers, we have crossed over the line into bondage.

The devil would love for you to choose to walk in weariness until you hit bottom. Satan wants you to lose heart so that you will not reap the beautiful harvest that is coming because you have sown good seed. The principle of sowing and reaping applies whether it is in our marriages, our children, our finances, or any other area. God guarantees the harvest when we sow the good that we want to reap (Galatians 6:7-8)! So, we must choose *not* to allow ourselves to be *yoked with the bondage* of *weariness*.

After Gabrielle was born, I became weary in my daily routine. Yes, I became weary with writing, singing, preaching, studying, reading, cooking — everything! I didn't want to do anything, and that is not me at all! I wanted to just curl up in a corner. I literally spent about a year physically exhausted, because I didn't understand that a spirit of weariness had consumed me.

People told me that I just had postpartum syndrome. Then doctors diagnosed me with chronic fatigue syndrome and all sorts of things. Well, the truth of the matter is I probably did have those things in my body. But I had a problem that was worse. I was in bondage to weariness and I was letting my physical man override my spiritual man. My spirit needed to take control of my flesh, but my *heart* had to make a choice.

One morning I woke up and made that *willful choice of the heart*. It was *more* than choosing to be happy. It was *more* than deciding to act and react differently. I determined in my heart that I would not allow my flesh to rule my spirit. I resolved at that moment to do whatever I needed to do to get my flesh under the control of my spirit. And when I made that choice *in my heart,* the Holy Spirit came right alongside me and helped pull me up out of the muck and mire of my weariness. (Psalm 18:16.)

I began to stand on the willful choice of my heart and allow the Holy Spirit to guide me practically. Then, as God's Word promises in Isaiah 40:29-31, I began to be strengthened in my spirit.

**He gives power to the tired and worn out, and strength to the weak. Even the youths shall be exhausted, and the young men will all give up. But they that wait upon the Lord shall renew their strength.**

**They shall mount up with wings like eagles; they shall run and *not be weary*; they shall walk and not faint.**
**Isaiah 40:29-31 (TLB)**

Are you tired and worn out? Do you feel like giving up? Are you in bondage to weariness? Jesus, the Anointed, came to break every yoke of bondage (Isaiah 10:27) — including the bondage of weariness! Don't lose heart and quit before you reap a wonderful harvest! Stop and get to the heart of the matter. Realize that God is waiting for you to make a *willful choice of the heart* — and that Jesus is saying to you:

**Take My yoke upon you and learn from Me, for I am gentle and lowly in heart, and you will find rest for your souls. For My yoke is easy and My burden is light.**
**Matthew 11:29-30**

# Praying With Power

*Father, You are the everlasting God, the Lord, the Creator of the ends of the earth. Thank You that You neither faint nor are weary and that Your understanding is unsearchable. (Isaiah 40:28.) Thank You, Father, that You never give up on me even when I become weary. Thank You that You care that my burden (yoke) has become too heavy for me and I can come to the Anointed One, Jesus, to break the yoke. Pour Your anointing oil on me now and destroy this yoke of weariness.*

*Father God, I make a willful choice of the heart to yield myself one-hundred-percent to You. Holy Spirit, I ask that You come as my helper as I walk out my freedom from the bondage of weariness. Thank You that now, because I have made a willful choice of my heart, I can be energized and revitalized through the power of the Holy Spirit and Your Word. I give you notice , Satan, that I refuse to become discouraged and lose heart, for I know that the Father God's harvest is guaranteed as I sow good seed. I choose to move forward with an attitude of expectancy in my heart. In Jesus' name, amen.*

## Taking Faith Action

Look up Isaiah 40:29-31 in several different Bible translations (if you have access to different translations such as: *King James Version, New International Version, The Living Bible, The Amplified Bible*, etc.). If you do not have access to different Bible translations from friends or your own library, try your church or even city library. Decide which translation you like best and *memorize* all three verses. After you *memorize* the three verses, *meditate* on them and put them into your heart. Speak them out loud! You cannot put a scripture in your heart without putting it in your mind first! These scriptures are power-packed promises of God's strength in your life to defeat weariness!

# 39
# Sweet Submission—Divine Order

**Wives, submit to your own husbands, as to the Lord.**
**Ephesians 5:22**

Every time I announce that I am going to minister on submission, I get a flood of disappointed looks. Oh, women, if we could realize the beauty of submission! Submission to our husbands enables us to be poured into and covered. Picture it this way — hold your right hand out with the palm facing outward, then make a fist with your left hand and place it behind your outstretched right hand. This is a picture of the husband/wife relationship.

The husband is in front of the wife, protecting her from enemy attacks; yet she is undergirding him — supporting him and watching the rear. When we are in these positions, the wife is still able to hear "from above" because the husband is not "over" her. The husband is hearing from the Father, leading and covering his wife, and holding off the attack of the enemy so that she can hear from the Father.

It is so important that we operate in the divine order God has established for our families. Our children need order, stability, leadership, and consistency. They need to know who is the final authority in their lives. There is so much peace in our families when we realize and respect our God-given place.

There is so much freedom when we operate as the wives that God has called us to be! The undergirding (supporting, strengthening, helping) of our husbands is absolutely vital so they can receive from the Father and then pour it into us. That is why we must make ourselves subject to our husbands — so we can receive from them!

Just as water is poured through a funnel, we must be "in line" to receive the love that our husbands are to pour into us. Then we can pour into our children!

As our husbands line up with the Father God and allow His love to flow through them, we will be in a position to receive as we make ourselves subject to them. I can hear some of you saying, "But what if my husband isn't allowing God to pour through him?"

I once heard that Billy Graham's wife made the statement, "It is not my job to change Billy. That is the Holy Spirit's job. It is *my* job to *love* Billy." Isn't that the truth? Many of us are so busy wanting and trying to change our husbands that we forget to love them. We need to put on our undergirding prayer warrior clothes and let the Holy Spirit go at it! God has shown me the power of taming my tongue and *allowing the Holy Spirit* to deal with my mate. All I had to be concerned with was *my* heart condition with the Father God and roll over the care of the situation on Him.

My precious husband Harry is Lebanese, and if you know their nature, they are strong and strong-willed! Therefore, when Harry and I were first married we ran right smack into a dilemma where our two strong personalities just couldn't see eye to eye. Harry wanted me to quit traveling and ministering because he missed me so much when I was gone. He wanted to be with me and for me to be at home. However, I felt the call of God *so strong* that I could not even see his point of view.

Harry was so troubled about my traveling that I finally told the Lord I just couldn't handle the conflict anymore. I said to Him, "Lord, if this call on my life is really from You, You are going to have to speak to him. I know Harry loves You and hears from You, and I am not going to say a word to him (this was tough!) If You don't speak to him and give him peace about my calling, then I will know I am supposed to stay home and not travel and minister anymore."

This was really hard for me to do and say (it took several months for me to come to that point) because all I had ever wanted to do was feel the anointing on my life and let it flow to other people. All I ever wanted to do (and will ever want to do) is serve the Father God and minister to others in His anointing. I told the Lord that I was willing to give up the very desire of my heart unless He did something. From that moment forth, I did not worry about it. I just let it go into the Father's arms.

Less than two weeks later I received a call from Harry while I was on the road. This in itself was somewhat unusual because I was usually the one who called him. However, this time Harry called me and said, *"Cheryl, God has spoken to me."* I had to act like I was surprised, "Oh really honey, what did He have to say?" Harry continued, *"The Lord doesn't speak to me this clearly that often, but when He does, I know it is Him. He told me that you were supposed to stay on the road ministering, and that if you come off the road for me that I will be standing before Him!"* Harry wasn't sure if God was going to come down here to speak to him or if He was going to call him home — but he said he didn't want to find out!

It is worth it to wait on God! It is worth it to let the Holy Spirit do the heart changing in your mate. Harry and I could have come up with fifty different compromises and not a one of them would have been as good as that! From that day forth, Harry didn't argue with me about traveling and he had peace in his heart.

You might be saying, "But what if he didn't hear God? What if you had to stop traveling and ministering — what if, what if?" That is where trust comes in — faith in the Father God to take care of you, your desires, your future, your life, and your family. When you really trust God, *He will do* the right thing for you!

The important part for us is that we make sure *our* hearts are pleasing to the Father. God's divine order in our family relationships is beautiful and *for our benefit*. The husband and wife are on the same level, but in *different* roles — the woman is not lesser — she is *different!* God has made a chain of command so that we can all be in the authority that He has designed for us — husbands submit to Christ's authority (Christ leads the man), wives submit to the authority of their husbands (husbands lead wives), and children submit to their parents (husband and wife lead the children).

Like the funnel we pictured earlier, as God pours into the husband, the husband pours into the wife, and the parents then pour into the children! We must get it all in order! Children struggle when there is strife and disorder, but they flourish when there is a godly chain of command which brings security and freedom. Godly freedom starts with the wife and mother getting lined up with God's Word and submitting her life to Him.

That is why submission is *so* beautiful! Submission is *freedom!* Submision is freedom to operate in the authority that God has given you — freedom to be poured into from your husband — freedom for you to funnel the things of the Father God into your children. So resign now and don't try to be your mate's Holy Spirit. Allow the Father God to do great and mighty things in and through your mate, and realize the power you have to undergird him in prayer. Your prayers for your mate are more powerful than you know. When I quit trying to be Harry's Holy Spirit and turned our conflict over to God Almighty, the Father God spoke to my beloved husband and kept me doing what He has called me to do. God will do the same for you!

## Praying With Power

*Father, I thank You that You have given us a model relationship for marriage through the relationship You have with Your Son, Jesus. I pray that _____ and I will share a mutual love. (John 5:20, 14:31.) I thank You, Father, that even*

*though _____ and I have different **roles** and that
we accomplish different **functions** in our marriage relationship
(John 10:17, 14:28, 17:4), You have created us equal and we are to
live in unity (John 10:30, 14: 9,11.) I ask now, Lord, that You will
help me to esteem my mate and express my love for him by being
of one will and purpose with him. Help me to show respect in
both attitude and action.*

*Father God, I pray that when we face conflict or difference of
opinion in any circumstance or situation, You will help me to
remember to let **You** deal with _____. Father, I ask
now that You release the spirit of intimacy over our marriage. In
the power of the Holy Spirit I undergird _____
and thank You that as we walk in Your anointing together, we will
be able to pour Your unconditional love and security over our
children so they can fulfill Your purpose for their lives. In the
mighty name of Jesus, amen.*

## Taking Faith Action

Write a letter to your spouse today. (If you are single,
write a letter to the Lord!) Share with him how much you
are glad that *he* is the man! (and the spiritual head of the
house). Take the time to esteem him and tell him the things
that you appreciate about him. Tell him you appreciate the
father he is to your children. Thank him for covering you
and the family spiritually, and tell him your desire is to be
submissive to him. Then you will be in a position to receive
from him what he has received from the Lord.

Share with him the hand illustration from the
devotional (or let him read it if he is willing) that shows a
picture of the marriage relationship. Take the opportunity
to talk about God's divine order in your marriage. Pray
through the prayer together and ask that the Father will
release the spirit of intimacy in your marriage. Children
need to see, hear, and feel this divine order in operation in
your home. They feel safe and secure when things are in
godly order.

# 40

# A Prayer

## by Dr. Betty Price

**The prayer of a righteous man is powerful and effective.**

**James 5:16 (NIV)**

I thank You, God every day for a godly home, godly husband, and godly children. I thank You that because we have made the Most High our habitation, no evil shall befall us and no plague will come nigh our dwelling. (Psalm 91.) I thank You that because we fear You and delight greatly in Your commandments, our seed shall be mighty upon the earth and they shall be blessed. Wealth and riches shall be in our house and our righteousness endures forever. (Psalm 112.) (I name each child.)

Thank You, Father, that my family has the wisdom to make every decision that they need to make today. I thank You for continued protection and provision for them. I thank You that they have sensitive spirits and alert minds and they will serve You all of the days of their lives from this generation until Jesus comes. We are a family that will represent You in this world by precept and example — spirit, soul, and body — in word and in deed. In Jesus' name, amen.

*Dr. Betty Price is the wife of Dr. Frederick K.C. Price and the mother of four children. She also has four grandchildren. Betty's greatest desire is to be an example of Jesus in the world. She enjoys her life as a wife and mother and serving the people of God.*

# 41

# One Choice at a Time

**Where is the man who fears the Lord? God will teach him how to choose the best.**

**Psalm 25:12 (TLB)**

Choices, choices, choices. Every day is made up of thousands of choices. We have to choose for ourselves, choose for our husbands, choose for our children, choose what we cook, choose what we clean. Women are just *made up* of choices! There is a little plaque that says, "A woman makes more decisions in the first hour of her day than the Supreme Court makes in a year." It's true! We have to make so many decisions. We do not need to back away from the choices, but take the authority that God has given us through His Word, line up our will with His Word, and make the right choices.

My whole life has been one big choice after another. Having children put even more choices before me! The greatest choice that I seem to be faced with right now is staying home more with our children and ministering less on the road. This past fall I was faced with the great question, "Should I stay home even more?" The children seemed to need me more than ever and so did Harry! I prayed about it and God gave me the clear picture that it was His will for me to stay home more at this time. I knew this was not just my decision, because I love to travel and minister on the road!

I canceled three months worth of dates in a row and began to cut back drastically on the dates following those three months. After about two weeks, Roman came and climbed up in my lap. (He's such a lover.) He said, "Mommy, I am so glad you are home. I need you to hold

165

me." I knew right then I had made the right choice and God had it all in control. Later on after picking Lil' Harry up from school, he told me in the car, "Mommy, I'm so glad that you are here." Those little statements carried a loaded punch! Our children need me. And Gabrielle doesn't have to say anything — the smile on her face tells me she is so happy to have me home.

Many times our choices are not easy. Choosing to stay home was certainly not easy for me. I have been traveling full-time for fifteen years. Yet God knows the entire plan and He knows what our children need. When we stay in tune with God's voice, we will know His will and our children's needs also.

Your choices may or may not include whether to stay home or not, but your choices do vitally affect your children, your family, and your home. The mother sets the tone in her home. If the home is chaotic and stressful, check the mother. If the home is peaceful and serene, check the mother. God has designed it that way! You might be saying, "I am not responsible for the mess in my house." Well, you may not have made it with your own hands, but you allowed it or it would not be there! This hits me right between the eyes, too — and I don't like it either! But I know that it is true. If I want my home to be godly and peaceful, I have to exercise my right to act, walk, and talk like God and bring that kind of spirit and presence into my home.

Therefore, choose to serve God! Many women have not dedicated to serve the Lord one-hundred-percent. That is the first choice you must make! (Joshua 24:15.) The choices you make rule the outcome of your life (which includes your children and home)! God will back you up when you choose Him first, and the Holy Spirit will help guide and direct you through every choice.

We have all heard the saying, "Live one day at a time." I believe we can take it one step further and live one choice at a time. We must take every choice that we are faced with and choose (by the power of the Holy Spirit) to do what is right and pleasing in the sight of our Lord! Every right *choice* we make, we are growing in obedience to our Father God. Remember, it was Jesus' obedience to go to the cross that gave us the *choice* of eternal salvation through His redemptive blood (Hebrews 5:8-9). What a beautiful choice we have made when we walk one-hundred-percent in the salvation of Jesus and power of the Holy Spirit! Thank the Father God for the ability to *choose!*

## Praying With Power

*Father, I know that You beckon me to* ***choose*** *life. (Deuteronomy 30:19.) I know that life is made up of a myriad of choices. I come to You now and give You my life. I give You one-hundred-percent of me. I* ***choose*** *to serve You, God. I give You all of my hopes, my dreams, and my desires. I choose to be like You, God. I choose to be pure. I choose to keep my tongue, and I choose to keep my temper. I choose to be happy. I choose to pray.*

*I thank You, Father God, that You are a good God and that You are looking for militant warriors in the spirit realm. I want to become the fighter that You want me to be so I will defeat the devil on a* ***daily*** *basis, not just when I get excited in church. Father, I thank You that because I fear (have reverence for) You, that You will show me how to always choose the best! Lord, I will be careful to give You the glory and the praise. In the precious name of Jesus, amen.*

## Taking Faith Action

Fill in the following blanks with three different areas where You need to make choices. Search the scriptures and find God's Word to stand on for each situation.

I choose to _____. Date: _____

I choose to _____. Date: _____

I choose to _____. Date: _____

# 42
# Plants and Pillars

**Then our sons in their youth will be like well-nurtured plants, and our daughters will be like pillars carved to adorn a palace.**

**Psalm 144:12 (NIV)**

As parents, it is easy to wonder whether or not we are training our children strongly enough in the Lord to be able to stand as "plants and pillars" in the years to come. Sometimes, it seems as though we are making no progress with them at all. Exasperation will many times whisper in our ears that we are failing as parents and all of our efforts are in vain. The devil wants us to fear failure. He wants us to give up and believe it is impossible to train our children to serve the Lord in such a godless society. Yet, we know that God has enabled us to do all things through Christ Who strengthens us.

In fact, Romans 9:14-17 (NIV) says, **Is God unjust? Not at all! For he says to Moses, "I will have mercy on whom I will have mercy, and I will have compassion on whom I will have compassion." It does not, therefore, depend on our desire or effort, but on God's** *mercy*. Wow! What a punch in the devil's face! Yes, we as parents do our part to train our children as God's Word has instructed us, and we rely on the *mercy of God*. We are to pray that the mercy of God will hover over our children (and our parenting!). With God's mercy we can teach and train our children to know and walk in the things of God all the days of their lives.

When Lil' Harry was younger, we made the mistake of using the television as a babysitter. Granted, we didn't allow him to watch ungodly programs, yet in a sense Lil' Harry became addicted to the stimulus of television. As he has grown older, this has been an area that has produced quite a battle for us. In reading back through the journal that I keep on Lil' Harry, there was a particular season (almost a year) that it was obvious the "television battle" was a problem in our house. I saw that every few pages I was declaring, "Today we're making a new rule — only one hour of television per day." Four years later, I am still occasionally declaring the same rule! When Lil' Harry is twenty years old, he will probably still be making a rule to challenge himself not to allow his flesh to be addicted to the stimulus of being entertained by someone else.

Have we failed? No, we made a mistake which presents a challenge. But God's mercy endures forever. His mercy covers my error, and we are seeing much improvement as we continue to *train* Lil' Harry.

There is a difference between raising flowers and training children. We can't just "water" children and watch them grow. We have to *constantly and consistently train* them. Instead of television let's substitute reading and studying the Bible together, praising together, or even dancing before the Lord together.

We must teach our children to be excited about and enjoy the stimulus of the Holy Spirit and the Word of God! As the Word of the Lord and the power of His Spirit grow in our children, we will see them walk in discernment and strength. As we are faithful to train Lil' Harry, we are seeing that he is truly learning to *guard his own spirit man.*

Nine-year-old Lil' Harry will now say, "I don't think we should watch that program." or "Mom, I checked out that comic book to see if there was anything demonic in it before I bought it." All the years of battling have been worth it! We are gaining ground! Don't give up — just keep on keepin' on! We must teach our children to guard their own spirit man so when we are not around, they will be able to discern and disarm evil through the power of the Holy Spirit.

## Praying With Power

*Father God, I praise You for You are a merciful God. I know that mercy is not merely a passive emotion, but an active desire to remove any cause of distress in others. Therefore, I thank You that Your mercy motivates You to remove the cause of distress in my life. I pray, Father, that Your mercy will hover over my children and the process of training them to be "plants and pillars" for You. I ask for wisdom from above and claim James 3:17 that says, "the wisdom that is from above is first pure, then peaceable, gentle, willing to yield, full of mercy and good fruits, without partiality and without hypocrisy." I welcome You, Holy Spirit, to help me teach my children to guard their own spirit man. In Jesus' name, amen.*

## Taking Faith Action

Take a few minutes and ask the Holy Spirit to help you come up with three *creative* ideas to do with your children. Use the Word of God and make them fun and exciting! Remember, children want interesting things to do! Substitute these creative ideas instead of television or even Christian videos. Gear these creative sessions toward teaching your children to guard their spirit man.

With Roman, I didn't make the same mistake with the TV. As a result his television time is much easier to control. There is no battle concerning the TV and he is so gentle to handle. Isn't hindsight wonderful?

"A smart person learns from their mistakes."

"A wise person learns from others' mistakes."

*Which one are you?*

# 43
# Mom's Got an Attitude...
# A Great One!

Strip yourselves of your former nature — put off and discard your old unrenewed self — which characterized your previous manner of life and becomes corrupt through lusts and desires that spring from delusion; and be constantly renewed in the spirit of your mind — *having a fresh mental and spiritual attitude;* and put on the new nature (the regenerate self) created in God's image, (Godlike) in true righteousness and holiness. Therefore, rejecting all falsity and done now with it, let every one express the truth with his neighbor, for we are all parts of one body and members one of another. When angry, do not sin; do not ever let your wrath — your exasperation, your fury or indignation — last until the sun goes down. Leave no [such] room or foothold for the devil — give no opportunity to him.

**Ephesians 4:22-27 (AMP)**

Did you know God is not only concerned with our actions toward our children, but also our attitude toward them? Our heart attitude will determine, motivate, and drive our actions. Proverbs 4:23 tells us to **keep your heart with all diligence, for out of it spring the issues of life.** So what does keeping your heart mean?

Keeping your heart means to value and protect (with the Word of God and the power of the Holy Spirit) your mind, emotions, and will. *Keeping your heart also involves choosing to have a good attitude!* (There's that "choosing" word again!) As a mom, your attitude toward the Father God, yourself, and your children (and spouse for that matter!) is of utmost importance.

Let's talk about your attitude toward yourself. Moms, it is so vital that you give yourself some "private time." You must *plan* time for yourself and not let the devil make you feel guilty for doing so. This is not pampering yourself — this is doing what the Word tells you to do. We get so hung up on doing God's work and being a good wife and mother that we forget to take care of ourselves! We get sick or tired (or both) and develop a bad attitude, bad figure, and bad self-image. We must have some time to refresh and reenergize.

I try to take time to do "nothing!" Usually after all the children are in bed and Harry is reading or watching TV, I try to go and take a relaxing hot bath all to myself — no kids! — and sometimes I listen to classical music while I bathe. This escape usually only lasts about fifteen minutes, but it can make me feel like a human again! (I know you can relate!)

A small amount of exercise can also make you feel so much better about yourself. Even if it is only fifteen minutes every day, it will boost your self-image. Your mood will lighten just because you are doing something for yourself, not for anyone else. The children will usually join in if you are doing a video with good God-filled music on it (like my aerobics videos!).

These brief "outlets" are significant in helping you maintain a *good attitude* toward yourself. You must remember you *are* somebody to God and you have His attributes and attitudes inside! As you allow His attitudes to come forth, you will see your children from a different perspective.

I was listening to Kenneth Copeland this past summer and he told how the Lord had reprimanded him in the area of his attitude toward his children. His story spoke to me so much. Kenneth talked about how we expect more out of our own children and have less patience with them than we do with other people's children. I have tried not to do that to my children every day since. It is difficult because we don't feel responsible for other children's futures, and yet we *do* feel responsible for the outcome of *our* children's lives. Therefore, many times we are much harder and much less fair with our own children. We magnify their sins and make the problem seem bigger than it really is when trying to make a point to our children. The Holy Spirit has really enlightened me and taught me regarding this unjust attitude toward our children.

Roman is such a sweet child that rarely will another child tattle on him. However, other children (especially Roman) will tattle on Lil' Harry, who is just as precious but very rambunctious. I have learned not to jump in and solve the problem by making Lil' Harry look like the bad guy — regardless of whether he was or not. Instead, I tell the children to go back and work it out. I give them the option to come back to me if they just cannot work it out, and I will decide then if punishment is necessary. I remind them to keep in mind that everyone involved could possibly be punished! It is amazing how much they can solve on their own! My children are benefiting from *my* change of attitude!

The Father God wants us to have a good attitude, especially toward our children. They are copying us! And we don't want a bunch of bad attitudes running around! In any area of your life that your attitude is bad, *choose* to have a fresh, new, Christlike attitude. (Ephesians 4:23.) Then don't let the devil waltz in with that old negative attitude when you are tested and tried — be done with it. (Ephesians 4:25.) If you need to get mad, get mad at the cause and not the carrier. Get mad at the devil! (Ephesians 4:26.)

Don't give the devil a foothold in your life by letting any bad attitude back in through your emotions. Guard your emotions carefully, because they are many times the

window the devil uses to sneak back into your life. Be wise
and stand firm! (Ephesians 4:27.) The Holy Spirit will help
you to change your heart attitude.

Remember the old saying, "If Mama ain't happy — ain't
nobody happy"! Choosing to walk in a good attitude will
make *your* life so much more wonderful — not to mention
your family's as well!

## Praying With Power

*Father God, I thank You for enlightening me about the
importance of my attitude in my own life and the way it affects
my children and my spouse. Holy Spirit, I ask that You help me
choose to have a good attitude. I pray that You will bring to light
every bad attitude I have in my heart. I realize that I am someone
special and I am able to walk in a Christlike attitude because of
Jesus who lives within me. Holy Spirit, help me as I choose to
guard my emotions and not allow the devil a foothold in my life
through a negative attitude.*

*Thank You, Father, that my children will be a reflection of the
choice I have made to have a good attitude. Thank You that they
too will choose to have a good attitude. I also commit to
"attending to Your Word" (Proverbs 4:20) and "keeping my heart
with all diligence" (Proverbs 4:23) so that I will continue to have
a good attitude. In Jesus' name, amen.*

## Taking Faith Action

*Memorize* Ephesians 4:22-27 and then meditate on these
scriptures to apply them in a practical way to any negative
attitudes you may have previously allowed in your life.
Give the devil notice that they are out the door! Then
choose to have a good attitude and fill up your heart with
God's Word.

# 44

# Taking Back Our Thought Life

...casting down arguments and every high thing
that exalts itself against the knowledge of God,
bringing every thought into captivity to the obedience
of Christ.

**2 Corinthians 10:5**

What we believe is a direct result of our thinking. If we
think wrong, we believe wrong. The Word of God is given
to us to straighten out our thinking. Because we women are
created more emotional, we must choose to take every
thought captive, *think* correctly, and put God first. We can
transform our thinking. How? By the renewing of our
minds (Romans 12:2) through reading God's Word,
listening to good teaching tapes, reading good God-filled
books, and listening to godly music tapes.

Thoughts come into our minds from two different
sources — the devil (outside) and from our spirit man
(inside). Therefore we must feed the inner man and build
our faith to dispel evil thoughts. Then we can hold fast and
choose to guard our thoughts, our tongues, and our
confessions. (Hebrews 4:14.) It is a battle, but we can have
victory in our thought lives!

Where is the battleground? In our minds! Jesus was
crucified in the place of the skull. (Golgatha means "place
of the skull.") So must we be crucified in the "place of the
skull." *The territory of uncrucified thought life is the primary
target of satanic attack in our lives*. We all want to live our
lives "risen with Christ," but we must first choose to be
"crucified" with Him, especially in our thought life.
(Colossians 3:1.)

Do you want to completely defeat Satan in your life? What kind of price are you willing to pay? To defeat Satan in your life, you must first be crucified in "the place of the skull" — your mind! You must be renewed in your thought life by thinking the Word of God.

My thought life has been a daily battle for me because I had been under subjection to fear and worry for so long! For example, I am constantly bombarded in my mind with worry thoughts regarding our children's future — what they will become in life. God told me it is not my responsibility to cause their futures to happen! It is His! It is my responsibility to teach them to hear and respond to God's voice. I have to consistently stand on what the Lord has told me and not give the devil an inch in tempting me to worry about our children's future. Our children's future is in His *big* hands!

Another area that is an ongoing challenge in my thought life is our children's safety, because of what we do for a living, who we are, and what we stand for. It has taken a tremendous amount of faith to relax and trust God in every situation. We safeguard as much as possible, then we trust God for what we can't or don't know to do. We have the right to turn over our children's safety to the Father God because He promises in Psalm 91 and other verses of scripture that the angels will protects us and our children. We cannot live in fear. Fear is not an option!

Some days on my way to pick up Lil' Harry or Roman at their schools, the devil will begin to lie to me. He will tell me that someone has taken Lil' Harry or Roman and they won't be there when I arrive. I immediately recognize these threats as lies from the enemy and I treat them as such!

The lies of Satan have no truth in them and I begin to speak the Word over the children, proclaiming liberty in the spirit realm for them. When I get to the school, I am sure the devil wishes that he had never started that lie. By the time I greet Lil' Harry and Roman, I have spoken so much Word and released so much faith into their lives that I am sure the devil's hands are tied *even* tighter than ever! Tie Satan up by speaking God's Word out of your mouth!

The enemy's ploy is to get you to leave thoughts uncrucified so that he will have access to you. Any area that is not crucified with Christ in your thinking, speaking, or actions is an area that is in spiritual darkness. Satan can enter in that darkness and attack you full force. Even your light can be in darkness.

Luke 11:35 says, **Take heed that the light which is in you is not darkness.** The light which is in you is the light of Christ. Proverbs 20:27 says, **The spirit of man is the lamp of the Lord**. God searches your heart with this lamp. Holy radiance illuminates from God's people, but willful disobedience (a harboring or holding onto sin) in any area can put "the light which is in you" in darkness.

Satan has a God-given right to the domain of darkness. By choosing to leave a certain area in darkness, you are giving Satan access to that area of your life. The devil can move in any area of darkness, even the darkness that still exists in a Christian's heart. I am not saying that a Christian can be possessed, but I am saying that satanic forces can come against you — especially in uncrucified areas. Uncrucified thoughts, cursing, R-rated movies, pornography, addictions of all kinds, pride, bitterness, anger — anything not under the control of the Holy Spirit — will open the door for a satanic attack. That is why it is so vital that we take control of our thoughts.

As a mother, it is imperative that I obtain victory in my thought life. Otherwise the devil would have me running around in circles worrying about our children. He loves to get you into fear about your children, so that you aren't releasing faith over and into your children. It all starts in the mind. Motherhood *does* start in the mind, and *your thought life* really can affect your children's future. Remember you *do* have the mind of Christ and you *do* have authority over every thought! Take charge of your thoughts this very hour!

## Praying With Power

*Most High God, I cast down arguments and every high thing that exalts itself against the knowledge of God. I bring every thought into captivity to the obedience of Christ. (2 Corinthians 10:5.) I call down every lying spirit in the name of Jesus, and I deafen my ears to the lies of the enemy. Lord, I choose to "be crucified in the place of the skull" — my mind. Father, I do not conform to this world, but I am transformed by the renewing of my mind, so that I may prove what is that good and acceptable and perfect will of God. (Romans 12:2.) Thank You, Father God, that I have the mind of Christ. Holy Spirit, teach me to **immediately** take thoughts captive and foil any plans Satan may have to build up a stronghold. Help me to take every thought that Satan meant for fear and turn it into an opportunity to release faith. In the mighty name of Jesus, amen.*

## Taking Faith Action

What areas in the "place of the skull" (your mind) do you need to crucify? Take a few minutes to allow the Holy Spirit to direct you to any areas that remain uncrucified in your life. Write down each area and then visually imagine nailing that area (written on a piece of paper) to the cross. Call forth your renewed mind in that area, in Jesus' name. Now go to the Scriptures and use a concordance or a topical scripture reference and find a verse (or verses) to take your stand against Satan. Be consistent and renew your mind as often as you need to until you walk in victory in each area.

Remember, you cannot fight thoughts with thoughts. You fight thoughts with *God-filled words!* Speak God's Word and every thought from the enemy will be brought to its knees.

# 45

# About Jesus Coming
## by Evelyn Roberts

**But the day of the Lord will come as a thief in the night.**

2 Peter 3:10

I think all of us who read our Bibles carefully and watch the things going on in the world have a feeling that the coming of Jesus or what we call the "rapture" is very close. Even when my children were small, over thirty years ago we taught them to be ready to meet Jesus, for none of us really knows when He will come.

One Sunday morning when Richard was about eight and Roberta was six, we were on our way to Sunday school and church services. It was January 1st. I said to the children, "Children, this is a brand new year and Jesus may come this year."

Roberta said, "Why will He come, Mother?"

Richard answered, "Because He wants to take us out of this wicked world, Roberta."

Roberta thought about that a minute and I'm sure she was thinking about her own little protected world, because she then said, "Oh, it's not a wicked world."

"Roberta, you just haven't been down town," replied Richard.

That's true! She hadn't been on the streets where wickedness reigned, and I'm glad she had a good opinion of our city. However, now conditions have changed. There is wickedness everywhere, not just on the streets. Our children must be protected every day, hour, and minute. They also must be taught to be ready to meet Jesus at any time.

We parents need to pray a wall of protection around our children and grandchildren, commanding Satan to stay away from our children in Jesus' name. More and more I find myself asking Jesus to keep my family covered with His blood to protect them from the attacks of Satan.

We need to talk again and again to our children about Jesus coming' to be sure they're not suprised when He makes His appearance.

# 46

# Unveiling the Crown

**Only be strong and very courageous, that you may observe to do according to all the law which Moses my servant commanded you; do not turn from it to the right hand or to the left, that you may prosper wherever you go.**

**Joshua 1:7**

As parents, we have such a great opportunity to impact our own children. Yet, not only will God use us with *our* children, He can use us to bless *other people's* children as well. We need to look for the open doors that God provides for us to be a witness for Him to other children. God gave me a wonderful occasion to share His truth with an entire elementary school full of children.

Lil' Harry goes to a public school. However, this is no ordinary public school. The principal is a Christian and nearly all of the teachers are Christians. At Lil' Harry's school they do not celebrate Halloween (Praise the Lord!). Instead they have a "Drug Free" week. I was asked to come and share with the student body something that I thought would help them.

I took my Miss America crown which is encased in a beautiful acrylic box and carried in a black velvet bag. When I stood up, I lifted the black velvet bag in the air and asked the children, "How many of you believe that this is a "magic box"? (Of course, those words "magic box" grabbed their attention.) The children responded with anticipation, "Yes, yes!" I then asked them if they thought the "magic box" could hold courage, perseverance, and strength. The children all agreed that they believed it could.

I then proceeded to tell them the story of my life. I

related to them how I had been in a car wreck as a child, was a cripple for six years, and how God had healed me. I shared with them how I was a poor little girl (who wore flour sack dresses) from Choctaw County, Mississippi, and how I had lost the beauty pageants for five years before I actually won the Miss America Pageant.

I expressed to them that in all the things I had been through, it had taken three ingredients to overcome — *courage, perseverance, and strength*. We discussed each ingredient. Then I asked them (over and over) to tell me the three ingredients necessary to overcome and they would shout with vigor, "courage, perseverance, and strength!"

After I finished sharing about my life I unveiled my crown. The children were so excited! There were "oohs and aahs" as they squealed with delight! (They were elementary age.) I then explained to them that it wasn't a "magic box," and it didn't hold courage, perseverance, and strength — but that my Miss America crown *represented* courage, perseverance, and strength. I told the children that we *do* have a "magic box" inside of us. It is a "magic box" that God has given us.

Then I asked all of the children to put one hand over their hearts. I said that in our "magic box" (our heart) God has put courage, perseverance, and strength and that each one of them may not have to overcome the things that I did in *my* life, but they too would have challenges to overcome. I encouraged them that they *were* able to pull from their "magic box" *courage, perseverance, and strength* to accomplish the goals in their lives.

It was such a beautiful time with the children. They were so attentive. I prayed that God would use my simple illustration to impact their lives. My prayer is that as those children grow up and come to know Jesus as Lord and Savior they will know that it is Jesus who holds the key to their "magic box," and *He* will equip them with courage, perseverance, and strength.

About a month later, I went back to the school and the Lord graciously allowed me to see what an impact the story had made. The children told me, with their hands over their hearts, that God had put a "magic box" in them and they could pull courage, perseverance, and strength from it. Praise the Lord for His creative ways to minister to His children!

Mom, the situations you must overcome may not be anything like mine. It could be the daily monotony of tons of laundry, keeping a house in order, or even loneliness. Your "mountain" can be anything. But one thing is for sure — *you too* will need courage, perseverance, and strength! The fact is, you know it is not a "magic box" that you contain in your heart. Your heart contains the Spirit of the Living God! We have a mighty Jesus in our heart Who holds the key to everyday problems — big or small.

Maybe you need to allow Jesus to unveil *His crown* in your heart. Jesus' crown of thorns represented the courage and strength He had to die for our sins. And the crowns Jesus will wear as the final trumpet sounds represent the reason we persevere. *Jesus Christ is coming again to reign as King of kings and Lord of lords forever.* (Revelation 19:16.)

## Praying With Power

*Almighty God, the Great I Am, the Alpha and Omega, I exalt You high above the earth. Jesus, **You** are crowned with many crowns, **You** are the Lamb upon the throne, the One Who is called Faithful and True. Thank You, Jesus, for choosing in courage and strength to go to the cross, suffer, and die for my salvation. Thank You that because I know You are coming again and that I will reign with You, I have strength to persevere.*

*Father, I pray that my children may see in me Your courage, Your perseverance, and Your strength. Let them learn that Jesus within our hearts gives us all that we need to see us through anything in life. Holy Spirit, I ask that You call to my remembrance the crown of Jesus that will give me hope when I may be tired, weary, or discouraged.*

*Thank You, Father God, for the hope that is set before me, that there is laid up for me the crown of righteousness, which You, Lord, the righteous Judge, will give to me on that Day (2 Timothy 4:8 ). In Jesus glorious name, amen.*

## Taking Faith Action

*Great verses to memorize!*

...praying always with all prayer and supplication in the Spirit, being watchful to this end with all *perseverance* and supplication for all the saints.

**Ephesians 6:18**

O God, You are more awesome than Your holy places. The God of Israel is He who gives *strength* and power to His people.

**Psalm 68:35**

Be of good *courage*, and He shall strengthen your heart, all you who hope in the Lord.

**Psalm 31:24**

Look up the definitions in a dictionary of the words *courage, perseverance,* and *strength.* Take the time to really understand their meanings. After you feel confident that you have an understanding of these important ingredients in your walk with God, sit down with your children and tell the "magic box" story in your own words.

Cheryl, I have "The Mommy Book!" Please pray for me as I take the challenge by God to become a more godly woman and in return, become a better mother. Please include me on your list of "Mothers on Our Knees" intercessors. I agree to pray every day for my children, my household, your children, your household, and thousands of other mothers' children and households. I commit to be a mother on my knees, fighting and changing things in the spiritual realm.

Name_____

Address_____

City _____ State _____ Zip _____

Phone Number _____

# Order Form —
# Cheryl Salem Library

If you would like more teaching materials or if you have a friend or loved one who needs help in a certain area of his or her life, just write for some of these materials.

| Books | Price | Quantity |
|---|---|---|
| *You Are Somebody* <br> (This is great for those who have developed <br> a poor self-image due to many different reasons.) | $5.95 | _____ |
| *A Bright-Shining Place* <br> (This is Cheryl's life story of how God raised <br> her from a crippled little girl in Choctaw County, <br> Mississippi, to Miss America in 1980. It will show <br> you what making the right choices can do for you!) | $6.95 | _____ |
| *ABUSE: Bruised but Not Broken!* <br> (Abuse of all kinds — physical, mental, emotional <br> — is found in many homes. This book can help <br> the abused and the abuser work through their past <br> and live a productive life with a good self-image.) | $2.95 | _____ |
| *How To Get a . . . BALANCED BODY!* <br> (A "show-and-tell" book of how to reduce <br> those troublesome spots and bring your body <br> into perfect balance by eating a balance of healthy, <br> nourishing foods — in moderation.) | $3.95 | _____ |
| *Royal Child* <br> (Cheryl's autobiography beginning with her <br> marriage to Harry Salem, their life together, <br> their ministry and their children.) | $5.99 | _____ |
| *The Mommy Book* <br> (A 31-day devotional for frazzled <br> moms with busy children.) | $8.99 | _____ |

**Mini-books**

| | | |
|---|---|---|
| *Health and Beauty Secrets* <br> (The tips Cheryl shares in this little book are <br> very practical in answering questions concerning <br> health and beauty. They can help you become <br> the best YOU that you can be!) | $ .75 | _____ |
| *Choose To Be Happy* <br> (This book is small, but powerful. It holds the <br> secret to being happy all the time. It's great for <br> people in all walks of life.) | $ .75 | _____ |
| *Simple Facts: Salvation, Healing and* <br> *the Holy Ghost* <br> (This book gives you the steps to take once you've <br> been saved, baptized with the Holy Spirit <br> [speaking in tongues], or healed, to make sure you <br> develop the way God wants you to.) | $ .75 | _____ |

## Music Projects

| | | | |
|---|---|---|---|
| *Choose to be Happy*<br>(All-music cassette with happy songs) | Cassette | $7.95 | _____ |
| *Ain't Nothin' Gonna Stop You Now*<br>(Motivational music) | Cassette | $7.95 | _____ |
| *The Music and Ministry of Cheryl*<br>(Miraculous testimony of Cheryl's healing, the story of winning Miss America, plus four songs.) | Cassette | $7.95 | _____ |
| *Living Proof*<br>(All-music cassette from "Richard Roberts Live" telecast, including: "Devil, Pick on Somebody Your Own Size," "I'm Not Lettin' Myself Get Down," and many more.) | Cassette | $7.95 | _____ |
| *With All my Heart*<br>(Inspirational tracks including: "You Are Somebody," "I Will Not Be Afraid," and "Don't Give In.") | Cassette | $7.95 | _____ |
| *My Heritage*<br>(Old favorites like "How Great Thou Art," and "Jesus Lord to Me/I Exalt Thee.") | Cassette | $7.95 | _____ |
| *Makin' My Dreams Come True*<br>(Upbeat and new, this recording comes from the heart with songs, "It's Too Soon," and title track, "Making My Dreams Come True.") | Cassette | $9.95 | _____ |

## Audio Teaching Tapes

| | | |
|---|---|---|
| *ABUSE: Bruised but Not Broken!*<br>(You will feel the healing anointing in this single audio cassette in which Cheryl deals directly with emotions and self-image that are a direct result of abuse of every kind.) | $4.00 | _____ |
| *Angels I and II*<br>(An awe-inspiring, two-tape series, based on Cheryl's own experiences with heavenly beings.) | $4.00 | _____ |
| *Breaking the Curse*<br>(Healing generational curses) | $4.00 | _____ |
| *Choices*<br>(Traveling the right path by following His will through life's difficult decisions) | $4.00 | _____ |
| *Courage*<br>(In today's society it takes more than just "want to" to accomplish what God has called us to do — thus this teaching tape on courage.) | $4.00 | _____ |
| *Depression*<br>(Overcoming the low points, moving on to a healthy and happy lifestyle) | $4.00 | _____ |

| | | |
|---|---|---|
| *Fear*<br>(How to overcome affliction in<br>your thoughts.) | $4.00 | _____ |
| *God's Principles to Prosper You*<br>(The importance of sacrifice in<br>all areas) | $4.00 | _____ |
| *Your Inheritance*<br>(How to pray more effectively for<br>God's will in your life.) | $4.00 | _____ |
| *How To Know the Will of God*<br>(Scripture-based teaching on<br>following His path for you.) | $4.00 | _____ |
| *How to Get Healed*<br>(God's best for you through His<br>healing power.) | $4.00 | _____ |
| *Male and Female, What a Difference*<br>(Simple differences that really matter) | $4.00 | _____ |
| *Nutrition*<br>(This single audio cassette is a must for<br>everyone who has bought the *Balanced Body* book.<br>Cheryl adds insights that will be a great addition<br>to what you learn from this book.) | $4.00 | _____ |
| *Proverbs 31 Woman*<br>(A single cassette teaching you God's<br>beautiful description of what a woman<br>can become at her best.) | $4.00 | _____ |
| *Rest: Ahh, Peace and Quiet*<br>(Learn the importance of taking<br>time out to be with the Lord.) | $4.00 | _____ |
| *Self-Image I and II*<br>(This wonderful two-tape set provides you with a<br>feeling of worthiness in being a child of God.) | $6.00 | _____ |
| *Submission and Obedience*<br>(Scriptural guidance for becoming<br>a true servant) | $4.00 | _____ |
| *The Anointing*<br>(How to become tuned-in and carry this special<br>touch from the Holy Ghost.) | $4.00 | _____ |
| *The Unstoppable Dream*<br>(The story of Joseph as a parallel of your dreams.) | $4.00 | _____ |
| *Thought Life: Crucified or Uncrucified?*<br>(How to have a healthy and<br>productive mindset.) | $4.00 | _____ |

## Aerobic Video Tapes

| | | |
|---|---|---|
| *Take Charge of Your Life with Cheryl*<br>*and Friends*<br>(High-impact aerobics video) | $15.00 (special)<br>Usually $19.95 | _____ |

| | |
|---|---|
| *Get Ready with Cheryl and Friends*<br>(Low-impact aerobics video) | $15.00 (special) _____<br>Usually $19.95 |
| *Cheryl's Defense Video*<br>(Nine self-defense moves<br>incorporated into aerobics) | $15.00 (special) _____<br>Usually $19.95 |

**Teaching Video Tapes**

| | | |
|---|---|---|
| *Depression*<br>(Overcoming the low points and moving on to<br>a healthy and happy lifestyle) | $14.95 | _____ |
| *Desperate Situations Require Daring Faith*<br>(Video coverage of Cheryl on concentrating on<br>your beliefs to get through the circumstances) | $14.95 | _____ |
| *God's Principles to Prosper You*<br>(Video coverage of Cheryl on the<br>importance of sacrifice in all areas) | $14.95 | _____ |
| *Your Inheritance*<br>(Video coverage of Cheryl speaking in Edmonton,<br>Canada, on understanding how to pray more<br>effectively for God's will in your life.) | $14.95 | _____ |
| *Magnificent Joy*<br>(Video coverage of Cheryl in Edmonton, Canada.<br>Watch the joy explode!) | $14.95 | _____ |
| *Male and Female, What a Difference*<br>(This hilarious video shows the<br>simple differences that really matter) | $14.95 | _____ |
| *Rest: Ahh, Peace and Quiet*<br>(Watch and learn the importance of<br>taking time out to be with the Lord.) | $14.95 | _____ |
| *Your Are Somebody*<br>(This wonderful video provides you with a<br>feeling of worthiness in being a child of God) | $14.95 | _____ |
| *The Unstoppable Dream*<br>(The story of Joseph as a parallel of your dreams.) | $14.95 | _____ |
| *Thought Life: Crucified or Uncrucified?*<br>(In this video Cheryl covers how to have a healthy<br>and productive mindset) | $14.95 | _____ |

**TOTAL AMOUNT ENCLOSED**                    $_____

Just clip this order form and mail with
your check or money order to:

**Cheryl Salem**
**P.O. Box 701287**
**Tulsa, OK 74170**

If you have any questions or comments, just write to
the address above or call (918) 298-0770. Please feel free
to include your prayer requests. Please print:

Name_____

Address_____

City _____ State _____ Zip _____

Phone Number _____